**Trans Care**

*(Continued on page 80)*

# Trans Care

## Hil Malatino

*University of Minnesota Press*
MINNEAPOLIS
LONDON

Published by the University of Minnesota Press, 2020
111 Third Avenue South, Suite 290
Minneapolis, MN 55401–2520
http://www.upress.umn.edu

Available as a Manifold edition at manifold.umn.edu

The University of Minnesota is an equal-opportunity educator and employer.

# Contents

# Surviving Trans Antagonism

## Aftercare

It's a new year: 2020. I have top surgery scheduled in two weeks. Friends are beginning to rally, sending books they love through the post for me to read while I'm stuck in bed, booking plane tickets to come help with domestic work that I'll be unable to do, volunteering to organize a post-surgery meal train, asking if I want to throw a farewell gathering to my tits (I don't). I'm a little nervous about the surgery, but I have so many loved ones that have been through different iterations of it. I know their stories, I know their scars, I know sitting up and standing is going to be rough for a while, that I need bendy straws to drink through and that I shouldn't really lift anything for a good long while.

I feel lucky to have all these practical manifestations of love in the form of care work coming through. A partner to help me through the healing process. Trans-inclusive insurance coverage. An employment situation that feels stable and relatively supportive. Friends with emotional, energetic, and financial resources. Manifestations of privilege, all. But also, this care web that is cohering around surgical aftercare has been delicately and elaborately woven for years, periodically (and always only partially) rent apart and repaired, made as much of loss as it is of sustaining linked threads. Its expansiveness is the reason for its resilience; the force of traumas psychic and physical is dispersed throughout its filigree of filaments. This is the secret power of the care web, which Leah Lakshmi Piepzna-Samarasinha theorizes as a crip-femme reworking of the integral anarchist concept of mutual aid (2018, 46)—from each according to their ability, to each according to their need. A resilient care web coheres through consistently foregrounding the realities of burnout and the gendered, raced, and classed dynamics that result in the differential distribution of care—for those receiving it as well as those giving it. A care web works when the work that composes it isn't exploitative, appropriative, or alienated. This is the gauntlet thrown down by any sustained attempt to collectively cultivate a care web: it challenges us to be deliberate, to communicate capacity, to unlearn the shame that has become attached to asking for, offering, and accepting help when we've been full-body soaked and steeped in the mythos of neoliberal, entrepreneurial self-making. It asks us to think carefully about what constitutes "good" care. It prompts us to sit communally with the question of how best to care for each other, with our differing abilities, idiosyncrasies, and traumas, with our hard-to-love thorns intact and sometimes injurious (to ourselves and each other).

This queer and trans care web has no center, but in some significant ways it has emerged because of the way the normative and presumed centers of a life have fallen out, or never were accessible to or desired by us in the first place. So many estranged and tangential relationships to birth or adoptive families, skepticism and proverbial allergies to normative familial structures, interpersonal, institutional, and professional shunning, exclusion, and ostracism. This is not the only synopsis I could provide—there's plenty of joy. But it would be foolish to deny that some of what binds us to one another is directly tied to the affective and practical disinvestment of the people and institutions we've needed—or been forced—to rely upon for survival. We have learned to care for one another in the aftermath of these refusals.

We talk about aftercare in the context of medicine, surgery in particular. It's a shorthand we use to mark the intensified vulnerability and differential physical capacity that one experiences after a physically traumatic event. We also speak of aftercare in relation to institutions—where children go between school and their return to a domicile, or what imprisoned subjects need upon release in order to "reintegrate" and prevent recidivism. It comes up in the context of BDSM, as well, as a way of recognizing that in the aftermath of an intense scene, some form of empathic connection and attending to one another is imperative. In all of these uses, care is necessary in the wake of profound recalibrations of subjectivity and dependency. We need care in order to heal from transformative physical and emotional experiences. We need it when the milieu we inhabit becomes radically reorganized. We need it especially when our lives fall in the gaps between institutions and conventional familial structures. Those gaps are worlds, and those worlds don't function without care work.

There are two linked definitions of aftercare, then. It is what needs to be provided in order to help a subject heal in the wake of massive upheaval and transformation, and it is what facilitates and supports emergence into a radically recalibrated experience of both bodymind and the world it encounters.

This feels like a trans concept. Whatever being trans is about, it's decidedly characterized by upheaval and emergence into a social world with shifting and shifted parameters. For many of us, surviving this process means committing to forms of healing that are unthinkable, indeed impossible, without care webs.

Aftercare is a concept that might move us beyond a focus on death, and in particular the spectacular homicides that continue to be enacted upon trans women of color, characterized by a form

3

of violence that Eric Stanley has termed "overkill" (2011, 1). The recurrent reference to such forms of overkill—operationalized through the memorials that compose the annual Transgender Day of Remembrance (TDoR) and familiar to most of us via routine posts about trans homicide on social media—has become de rigueur in social justice spaces and circulates as a form of virtue signaling, particularly among White folks on the left. As queer legal theorist Sarah Lamble points out, these necropolitical citations are too often "deracialized accounts of violence" that "produce seemingly innocent White witnesses who can consume these spectacles of domination without confronting their own complicity in such acts" (2008, 24). When such mentions of overkill are deracinated, they take part in a troublingly equivocal and definitively nonintersectional account of trans oppression. When race *is* mentioned, it is often as a means of performing an affective investment in trans of color survival that nevertheless evades considerations of complicity.

Poet and theorist Cam Awkward-Rich highlights the ethical vertigo that structures such forms of memorialization, writing that they are shaped by two "general claims: that it is important to keep the memory of individuals alive—to keep them with us—and that each entry on the list of the dead is an injustice" (2019). He calls our attention to the fact that such memorialization, focused on the brutal fact of death, misses the point: "What is unjust is everything that preceded the end. What is unjust is the terms of living. There is something deeply unsettling, that is, to the insistence that someone ought to be alive in a world that did little to support that life" (2019).

When we shift our attention from the brutal fact of death to the injustice that gives rise to trans arts of survival, we are forced to grapple with questions of complicity and care. What could have been done differently? In what ways have we been actively contributing to the unlivability of multiply marginalized trans lives? What ethos—what practice of living otherwise—might enable more liberatory forms of trans existence? What practices of care might ensure trans flourishing? What are the barriers we currently encounter as we attempt such care praxis? How do we destroy or surpass them?

In what follows, I try to provide a richer description of these barriers, prompted by the conviction that tarrying with them a while might bring us to a better understanding of how to work with and through them. I want our care webs to be as resilient as possible, which means I need to understand when, where, and how they come to tear. These webs so often begin to shred, or intensify in their desiccation, when we admit out loud that we're trans, when we come to that significant caesura in a life. We lose family, friends, jobs, and our mooring in various social worlds. Aftercare is about how we live through what comes after this rending of webs.

A minimal definition of community might be this: folks who are reweaving.

In what follows, I do my best to ground myself in the everyday rhythms of the trans mundane in order to think through some of the materials, textures, and methods at work in this reweaving. I begin with meditating on the role care plays in the affective and political economies of the present moment, when trans lives are recurrently and brutally utilized as a political wedge issue in order to consolidate horrifyingly ascendant forms of ethnonationalism and the ongoing violence of neoliberal austerity. This produces forms of hypervisibility that wear us out, that cultivate hyperalertness and anxiety that, for so many of us, make getting out of bed and getting through the day difficult.

I'm interested in how we survive this, how we cultivate arts of living that make us possible in a culture that is alternatingly, depending on where you're at and who you are, either thinly accommodating or devastatingly hostile. How are we showing up for each other, and how come it sometimes feels so hard to do so? The language we have to describe exhaustion in the context of coalitional political work—burnout, compassion fatigue, vicarious trauma, self-care—doesn't quite grasp the complicated reality of working to make one another's (deeply interwoven) lives more livable in the broader context of institutional disinvestment and systemic harassment and discrimination that produces mutually resonant forms of traumatization and triggering. I think through how we might begin to move beyond the rhetoric of burnout and toward a logic of postscarcity in order to do justice to the methods of collective support that we have spent decades actively inventing and elaborating—and to render them more robust.

This necessitates really grappling with questions of care—how we understand it, how we measure it, how we account for it. For far too long, both hegemonic and resistant cultural imaginaries of care have depended on a heterocisnormative investment in the family as the primary locus of care. Let me use a colloquialism from my years in the South: *this ain't right*. Another colloquialism: *this shit is fucked*. To state the obvious: some of us have okay relationships with our families of origin, but a whole lot of us don't. A lot of us don't have families, full stop. We lost them somewhere along the way. They rejected us. We had to escape them in order to survive. We cobbled together some network of support, some other kind of care web, instead. We might call that a family, too—a family of choice, a family constructed through consent rather than accident and forced relation. But whatever our relationship to family—the word, the construct, the ongoing practice of building one—it's also obvious that our ability to flourish is reliant on forms of care that outstrip the mythic purported providential reach of the family. One thing—maybe the main thing—I'm trying to do here is think about what care actually looks like in trans lives. This means decentering the family and beginning, instead, from the many-gendered, radically inventive, and really, really exhausted weavers of our webs of care. When I write about transing care in the central portion of this little book, this is what I'm writing about. Transing care also means grappling with the fact that the forms of family and kinship that are invoked in much of the feminist literature on care labor and care ethics are steeped in forms of domesticity and intimacy that are both White and Eurocentered, grounded in the colonial/modern gender system (Lugones 2007). Acknowledging this intensifies the necessity of decentering dominant imaginaries of how care labor does and should operate and also raises the questions of how differentially racialized trans subjects are oriented toward questions of care in the context of kinship and kin-making.

I have also felt compelled to write about trans archives and hirstoricity, because a common feature of trans arts of cultivating resilience has to do with turning to the historical record for proof of life, for evidence that trans lives are livable because they've been lived. Care enters here, as well, because we turn to the archive for the purposes of support and self-care, but in that turning we are also confronted with the ineffability and alterity of these personages—many of them only a trace, a suggestion, a minor life only lightly embroidered upon in the scraps to which we have access. How do we care for these traces of past lives that haunt us in ways that are loving, insofar as they offer a balm through providing evidence of past trans flourishing and joy, and terrifying, because they testify to the conditions of intensive violence that these subjects lived within and through? How do we care for these ghosts that take such care of us?

Finally, I look to the phenomenon of medical denials of care, with which too many of us are familiar. The most elaborate manifestations of trans care work have emerged from the communal history of redress in the wake of such denials. From the community support group to the trans newsletters detailing supportive medical professionals and gender hacks to the Yahoo newsgroups and listservs of the early internet to current forms of transition-related crowdfunding, we have a long history of building solidarity as a direct response to the vagaries of the medical-industrial complex. A text on trans care couldn't *not* address this, as it's the crucible through which so much of our connectivity has emerged. I don't know what trans care webs would look like without this ensemble of practices—and I don't particularly want to imagine it.

## I REALLY DON'T CARE DO U?

In June 2018, photographers wrangled photos of Melania Trump entering a black SUV in McAllen, Texas—a site deeply affected by the Trump administration's family separation policies—wearing a thirty-nine-dollar olive drab jacket from fast-fashion giant Zara emblazoned with white scrawled text that read, infamously, "I REALLY DON'T CARE. DO U?" In the media shitshow that followed, much was made of this phrase. Was she commenting on the policies wrenching apart migrant families entering the United States? Did she truly not care about the well-being of those families, especially the children who are directly, radically, and negatively affected by such policies, interned in dismal and unsanitary conditions for cruelly long periods of time? Was it evidence of a newly cultivated flippancy in relation to liberal and left-wing news media?

Whatever Melania's intentions were, the jacket could not just be a jacket. The scene was far too semiotically rich for that. Even buying the jacket is symptomatic of Melania's uncaring, given Zara's well-documented history of labor abuses—labor abuses that have driven workers in Turkey to sew pleas for help into the clothing they produce (Girit 2017).

The jacket felt like a hyperdistillation of the callousness of Trumpism, a glib summation of the kind of affective orientation one would need to cultivate in order to speed headlong into the apocalypse, screamingly denying climate change, cultivating xenophobia, White supremacy, and neofascism, laying the juridical groundwork for the rollback of queer and trans rights and abortion access, metastasizing Immigration and Customs Enforcement (ICE), proliferating carceral archipelagos. A complete disregard for questions of social justice, a shrug in the face of compounding natural-cultural disasters, and, at the center of this whirlwind, a four-letter word that has, in some ways, come to stand in the place of traditional partisan orientations: care. Do you care or don't you? Melania doesn't, obvi. Melania the metonym, the well-groomed avatar of the neoliberal far right, but also, within some leftist fantasies of rescue, the trapped and long-suffering wife in need of saving from the Big Orange Bully. As long as Melania can be convinced to care, there might be hope. It's a matter of convincing her to regurgitate the bait she took, to extract the lure from her mouth, to make an escape, to cultivate disloyalty to her abusive captor, to heal from her Stockholm syndrome. If she can only manage this, she might be convinced to *care* again. She might shrug off the yoke of glib dismissal and cultivated detachment and rediscover empathy and human warmth once more. It's worth noting that the avowedly feminist clothiers at Wildfang produced a T-shirt by way of response that read, in the same font, "I REALLY CARE. DON'T U?" and that their website description for the product begins "Hey Melania." Call out or call in?

Care is deeply political. Its circulation as an affective shorthand for leftism—crucially consolidated in the discursive maelstrom surrounding Melania's jacket—alerts us to this. To stand on the right side of history is to care. To be committed to social justice is to care. Self-care is imperative for those in the political

9

trenches of the left—we spend so much time caring for others we forget to care about ourselves, but we can't care for others effectively if we don't attend to our own needs sometimes. Self-care is warfare, after all, as Audre Lorde (1988) reminds us. We actively care for folks—as social workers, sex workers, teachers, parents, service workers, nurses, nonprofit hustlers—but we also care about others in the abstract. We are able to pragmatically prioritize the greater good; we are not, ostensibly, wholly dominated by the vicious id of self-interest. We are able to place ourselves in another's shoes: to care is to empathize enough to grasp and service the needs of another, and to do so willingly. Care is supposedly uncoerced, given freely, by a person with enough agency to decide that they will expend resources—energetic and/or financial—on an other, in the interest of and in service to an other or others.

Do u care or don't u? In the affective economies of the present, this might be the animating political question.

## Defined Out of Existence

Fast-forward four months. It's Sunday. I'm in bed. My partner brings me coffee, tosses me my phone so I can look at the news. And there it is, in the *New York Times*. The Headline: "'Transgender' Could Be Defined Out of Existence under Trump Administration." I read in shock, even though I should know better, even though I *do* know better than to be this nonplussed. The strategy being deployed by the Department of Health and Human Services under Trump—interpreting gender as reducible to biological sex, where biological sex is wrongly understood to be radically dimorphic and grounded, fundamentally and irrevocably, in the aesthetic appearance of the genitals at birth—is old hat. I lived and taught in the southern United States for years; I've listened to conservative politicians repeat this idiocy over and over again in order to attempt to push through transphobic legislation. I've always balked at this reasoning, in large part because I have an intersex condition (partial androgen insensitivity syndrome) that means my own body was never—at the biological level and, indeed, at the genital—neatly "male" or "female." The effort to rhetorically recode biology as binary is a direct denial of the biological diversity and exuberance of bodies, and the biologists already know this.

The impact of the headline comes, I think, from the phrase "defined out of existence," which conflates the nominal with the existential in a way that seems to grant a bit too much force to the power of discourse. To be made juridically illegible is a form of erasure and exclusion, to be sure, but it's not as if we'll stop actually existing on account of how we're interpellated by Health and Human Services. Though I teach, often, about the historicity, contingency, and politics at play in the emergence of trans identities, there's something ineffable about transness that exceeds the terminological and the identitarian. Surely there have always been other bodies that move in the way ours do; surely other epochs have known the wildness and beautiful dissidence of trans gestures. I want to toss my phone across the room. But instead, I read the article out loud to my partner, cuddled next to me in bed, beneath a pink duvet with little black and white polka-dotted ponies on it. Then, we make breakfast and clean the house—two trans mascs in love, in sweatpants, continuing on with the business of existence, in all its banality, on an autumn Sunday. I rake up leaves and think about what the redundant alarmism of the news cycle is doing to my adrenals. I think about how acculturated I've become to being discursively defined out of existence, and not just by conservative administrations.

A couple of days later, I enter the women's, gender, and sexuality studies seminar room at Penn State. I work here. Issues of *Signs* ranging back to the mid-1970s line the walls. I remember interviewing here, being sat in this room between meetings (so many meetings—the endless interview stream that is the audition for the tenure track) and scanning the shelves, feeling comforted by the gravitas these back issues lent the space, the sense of material feminist history that bound volumes that you can actually hold in your hands affords. The collection, of course, peters out towards the end of the 1990s, on account of the internet. I realized that the feminist print that is present and tangible in the room ends at the moment that coincides with the emergence of "transgender" as a shared and increasingly legible way of referring to trans folks, outside of (or, more accurately, to the side of) more strictly medicalized nomenclatures. I know that there is no robust literature on transness on these shelves.

*The feminist history I can grasp is a history where I am only obliquely present.*

I do know that, somewhere in the stack, there is Donna Haraway's essential two-part essay from 1978, "Animal Sociology and a Natural Economy of the Body Politic," where she asserts, in a ground-clearing moment that makes space for what we now call feminist science and technology studies, that "women know very well that knowledge from the natural sciences has been used in the interests of our domination and not our liberation" (22). Trans people know this, too, deeply. The false claim of biological sexual dimorphism gets weaponized, over and again, in ways that aren't only, or aren't just, misogynist but strategically wielded against trans folks to indict us as deceptive, false, constructed, fake, bad mimes, impersonators. The Real is Biological is Dimorphic.

I'm leading a graduate seminar in gender and sexuality studies the semester that I'm defined out of existence. Some of the students I'm working with are reeling from a transphobic screed published by a tenured faculty member at the same institution and are, in a sense, seeking refuge from his course by studying with me. Some of these students are trans, some aren't; most all of them have a kind of fragility and brittleness to them, the kind of affect you cultivate when you can't trust the world to see you, to hold you. I'm particularly attuned to the ways this fear manifests among those students who are trans-identified. Most of us, of necessity, have cultivated a deep skepticism of cis professors and university administrators (and, let's be real, of cis people more generally). We're always waiting for the other shoe to drop, for the microaggression to hit; it's a state of hyperalertness that's exhausting and exacerbated by the fact that we're consistently told we're too sensitive, that our frustrations are outsize in relation to the slights we perceive. I accept the fact that these students have come to work alongside me, in part, because I won't misgender them, at least not consistently or intentionally. I certainly won't wield the rhetoric of "free speech" and "reasoned debate" as a justification for doing so. I won't attribute the insistence of students to be referred to by the correct gendered pronouns as an example of "toxic call-out culture." I won't do these things because I understand that they render the classroom an unnecessarily harmful space. I won't do these things because, whatever my critiques of identity and the institutional regulation of gender might be, that doesn't prioritize theoretical rightness over the well-being of actually existing human beings. I won't do these things because I understand how your throat seizes up when you're consistently misrecognized in ways that mark you as aberrant, inauthentic, hysterical—an irrational paragon of the rights of the particularly minoritized, to be appeased, perhaps, but never taken seriously. To be dismissed as one who does "grievance studies." When I was in graduate school, I was subject to this line of reasoning, as well—a dismissal of intersectionality arrived, from one of my committee members, in the form of his often-repeated phrase "But who will speak for the left-handed Lithuanian lesbian?" I cringed then; I cringe now.

I *am* aggrieved. These students *are* aggrieved. Grievance is not adequate grounds for dismissing a critique. More to the point: one might actually learn something by studying grievance, particularly if the form of grievance they are quickly moving to dismiss as unworthy of study is one that seems minor. Misgendering, when done by a cis person, might be a small misstep made in the course of a day—unfortunate, perhaps, but really no big deal. Misgendering, when it happens to a trans person, is equally routine, but the felt impact couldn't be more disparate. Because when it happens to us, we are being told that we, as Eva Hayward so powerfully puts it, "don't exist" (2017, 191). Being told we don't exist—despite all the obvious indicators that we, in fact, do—operates as an "attack on ontology, on beingness" (191). This form of ontological attack slips too easily into a justification for harm; it is a way of marking trans populations as subhuman—thus expendable, disposable, dismissible, even killable. Because it has happened to most of us regularly, for quite a long time, each time it occurs resonates down the long corridor of a life, echoing each other moment wherein this denial of existence has happened. This is the case for all of us, I'd wager, except those who are particularly good at forgetting, those who have cultivated it as a special talent, a superpower. Forgetting: another trans art of survival.

In seminar, a few days after The Headline, while discussing C. Riley Snorton's then-new *Black on Both Sides* (2017), the conversation inevitably, inexorably turns to that *Times* story. What we talk about, perhaps more than any other aspect, has to do with the callousness of the alarmist tone the lede takes. Doesn't the editorial staff understand that we're living in a state of affective oversaturation, dominated by ambient angst and hyperalertness?

## Fall Out Boy Is Trans Culture

The header image that ran alongside this *Times* article is a protest shot. The two figures most clearly in focus, at the front of the crowd, appear to be trans masculine (though I have no idea how either one identifies). Both are light-skinned, with dark hair and dark eyes. One has a trans pride flag tied around their neck, thick black-rimmed glasses, a slightly fuzzy shaved head, and a septum piercing. The other is slightly taller, with a grown-out fade (left shaggy on top, the exact same haircut I sport while writing this), and they are wearing a Fall Out Boy shirt. This last detail matters. For me, this shirt was a punctum, for sure—that photographic detail that doesn't belong to the conventions of the image-genre (this is a protest image—it's giving us sad-mad and righteous trans folks in a moment of mass resistance); it could have been any shirt, but it was *this shirt,* and "that accident . . . pricks me (but also bruises me, is poignant to me)" (Barthes 1981, 27).

Fall Out Boy fandom is a strange beast that I've never quite been able to comprehend; I was too old, too feminist, and too much of a political punk by the time they became popular to be at all interested in them, given that their fan base, in the mid 2000s, seemed to be composed primarily of White suburban tweens and teens. Kelefa Sanneh, reviewing a 2007 show, sets the scene for us: "It was a breezy Tuesday night here at the Nikon at Jones Beach Theater, and the stands were filled with screaming teenagers and a few nonscreaming parents. . . . All night long you could hear the high, trebly sound of teenage adulation, and if you went anywhere near the teeming merchandise tables, you could hear a different but not unrelated sound: cha-ching!" They rose to fame after some years of languishing in the Chicago-area punk and hardcore scene, in other bands (notably, their drummer was in an antiracist political hardcore band named Racetraitor who released an album entitled *Burn the Idol of the White Messiah* in 1998). Feminist rock critic Jessica Hopper, a veteran of the Chicago punk scene, writes about the ascendancy of mainstream-radio-friendly emo in a scathing 2003 essay in *Punk Planet* entitled "Emo: Where the Girls Aren't," noting that "as hardcore and political punk's charged sentiments became more cliché towards the end of the 80s and we all began slipping into the armchair comfort of the Clinton era—punk stopped looking outside and began stripping off its tough skin only and began to examine its squishy heart instead, forsaking songs about the impact of trickle down economics for ones about elusive kisses. Mixtapes across America became laden with relational eulogies—hopeful boys with their hearts masted to their sleeves, their pillows soaked in tears. Punk's songs became personal, often myopically so" (2015, 15). There was a gender politics to this sea change: the women that appeared in the lyrics of those bands that came to represent this shift in the public eye—Dashboard Confessional, Brand New, Something Corporate, and, yes, of course, Fall Out Boy— were mere ciphers for sexist sentiment. Hopper writes that "girls in emo songs today do not have names. We are not identified beyond our absence, our shape drawn by the pain we've caused . . . our actions are portrayed solely through the detailing of neurotic self-entanglement of the boy singer—our region of personal power, simply, is our impact on his romantic life" (16).

This means, also, that Fall Out Boy belongs to a genre that places the heartaches, trauma, and heroism of boys at the center of each song; their charm hinges on the overwrought purple prose of front man Pete Wentz, who—at least in his younger years— possessed a kind of *Tiger Beat* by way of *Maximum Rocknroll* charm; he was juvenile, erudite, and the public persona he performed was honestly kind of campy. Their most well-known tracks are anthemic in the ways that Broadway musicals are; they consistently shift between baritone and falsetto registers

(Patrick Stump, their guitarist and lead vocalist, has an undeniably impressive upper range); and they repeatedly violate the generic conventions of emo-pop-punk—which hinge on the performance of a certain kind of emotional earnestness, a direct delivery of a sad boy's wrought internal monologue on the vagaries of romance—in order to inject a heftier dose of the theatrical. All of this was part of why I didn't—and don't—particularly enjoy listening to them. But I'm not a teenage trans masc. And I kept coming back to that image, kept thinking about the T-shirt, kept wondering whether or not there might be a kind of trans specificity to Fall Out Boy fandom.

I agree with Hopper—emo is a genre where girls have nearly zero specificity or particularity. It is a genre where they are mere romantic tropes—heartbreaker, psychotic ex, current obsession. The male protagonist possesses all of the emotional complexity. He is the definitive lead in the pas de deux. But, for AFAB (assigned female at birth) folks, the utter irreality of the feminine might be deeply appealing. It's much more difficult to resonate with (or be triggered by) a thinly wrought love interest who, as Fall Out Boy's career-making song "Sugar, We're Goin Down" puts it, is "just a line in a song," especially when that figure is juxtaposed with the narrator's self-proclaimed "loaded God complex." The boy at the center of a Fall Out Boy track is gamely and selfishly working his way through minor emotional devastations, centering his sexuality (however problematic or cringeworthy these narratives are, replete with boys "wishing to be the friction in your jeans"), and being eminently braggadocious and narcissistic—he'll be your "number one with a bullet." He's stationed directly at the center of a completely solipsistic universe. No matter how insufferable this kind of guy is in reality, I would have killed for a fraction of his swaggering self-confidence as a kid. Repeated drafts from that reservoir might have made getting through high school just a little bit easier.

I really, really do not enjoy listening to Fall Out Boy, but I do my best to empathize with this baby trans masc, regardless. I dilate on what might lead them to love a band I loathe, on how that band might speak to transmasculine fantasies and desires, even if I find them politically and ethically suspect. This, too, is all about care. Sometimes young trans guys annoy me in precisely the ways that Fall Out Boy annoys me. But I want them to have their clueless and self-involved boyhoods. I want them to be able to take the long road through navigating toxic masculinity, to sloppily grapple with it the way that other boys get to do. I want them—I want all of us—to maintain the kind of wide-eyed silliness and unabashed enthusiasm that we associate with childhood but that, in fact, only the most privileged and unharassed kids get to experience. I don't want trans kids entering adulthood already suspicious, already untrusting, waiting for the other shoe to drop, already skeptical, burnt out, tired. I want them to experience what Justin Vivian Bond calls the "luxury of normality"—an experience of youth where they are "no more, no less interesting than anyone else. No more exciting or exotic than any other healthy high school kid . . . able to experience the same dramas, heartaches, and joys that any other kids would have to go through, no more and no less" (2011, 132–33). I want them to have trans elders to turn to, and I want them to have the chance to become trans elders themselves.

# Beyond Burnout

## "Voluntary Gender Workers"

Rupert Raj is a still-living trans elder, and he's *been* tired. He's been doing trans care work since 1971—the year he began to transition, at age nineteen. At the 2016 Moving Trans History Forward conference at the University of Victoria, British Columbia, Raj participated on a "Founders" panel, as one of a handful of trans movement and advocacy lifers. He summarized his experience with a not-so-brief timeline, schematizing the bulk of his life's work as such:

> From 1971 until 2002, I was a voluntary gender worker (or professional transsexual), now known as a "trans activist," providing information, referrals, education, counseling, and peer support to transsexuals and cross-dressers and their partners and families across Canada, the US, and abroad. I also offered free education, doing training workshops, offering newsletter and magazine subscriptions on transsexualism, gender dysphoria, and gender reassignment to psychiatrists, psychologists, psychotherapists, social workers, physicians, and nurses, as well as researchers, academics, educators, students, lawyers, policy makers, and politicians.

I was struck by the occupational equivalences with which he began this description and the temporal dimension he assigned to them—his movement from "voluntary gender worker" to "professional transsexual" to "trans activist." He claims the term "voluntary gender worker" for himself, and it's likely that he coined it. He started a consultancy group that he dubbed Gender Worker in 1988 and ran a short-lived newsletter for "gender workers" called *Gender NetWorker* around the same time. Though the newsletter only lasted for two issues, the impulse behind it—to produce a resource for trans folk who found themselves doing mostly unremunerated advocacy work—speaks both to the absolutely common and widespread phenomenon of "voluntary gender work" (anecdotally, I don't know any trans people who *don't* do this work) and to the dearth of communal, institutional, and social support for such work, which makes such labor ultimately unsustainable and typically deleterious in the long-term.

It's not surprising, then, that he began his talk with a frank admission that he'd recently taken a leave from his job as a psychotherapist at Sherbourne Health in Toronto, where he counseled trans, nonbinary, two-spirit, intersex, and gender nonconforming folks as part of Sherbourne's comprehensive trans health program. In his own words: "I've been on an indefinite medical leave since last May due to, ah, work-related stress, an unhealthy workplace culture, chronic burnout, vicarious traumatization, clinical depression and generalized anxiety requiring psychotropic medication and ongoing psychotherapy." This allied set of causes, symptoms, and manifestations, however, is not at all unfamiliar to him. Back in 1987, in an issue of *Metamorphosis*—a bimonthly magazine for trans men that ran from 1982 to 1988—he penned a feature editorial entitled "BURN-OUT: Unsung Heroes and Heroines in the Transgender World," which offers up a list of fourteen trans men and women who, after many years of unpaid advocacy work, left their posts or ceased to do such work. He concludes this list with a discussion of his own experience: "I have been serving the transgender community in a variety of capacities (administrator, educator, researcher, counselor, peer supporter, local convener, public relations/liaison officer, networker, editor, writer, chairman of the Board—you name it, I've been it) for the past 15 1/2 years *without any form of monetary remuneration whatsoever*" (1987, 3).

What Raj describes is something more intense and insidious than burnout. Burnout, as a mental health diagnostic, emerges from organizational psychology literature in the late 1970s and early 1980s that was primarily concerned with decreased rates of job satisfaction and declining workplace productivity. In the classic text on the phenomenon penned by social psychologist Christina Maslach, one of the women credited with "discovering" burnout (alongside coresearcher Kathy Kelly Moore), *burnout* is defined as follows:

> A syndrome of emotional exhaustion, depersonalization, and reduced personal accomplishment that can occur among individuals who do "people work" of some kind. It is a response to the chronic emotional strain of dealing extensively with other human beings, particularly when they are troubled or having problems. Thus, it can be considered one type of job stress. Although it has some of the same deleterious effects as other stress responses, what is unique about burnout is that the stress arises from the *social* interaction between helper and recipient. (1982, 3)

There are a number of founding assumptions worth troubling in this articulation of burnout. The first is that burnout is, specifically, a stress related to employment and thus a problem for both employers and employees to recognize and attempt to manage. Another is that it is characterized by a fundamentally bifurcated and unequal energetic exchange, where the roles of *helper* and *recipient* are clearly demarcated, hierarchical, nonfungible, and nonreciprocal—the relationships that produce burnout are not horizontal or nonhierarchical, peer-to-peer. As an extension of this logic, burnout is conceptualized as a personal—

individualized—rather than a communal issue, one that affects, in particular, those in the so-called (and often feminized) helping professions. Another extension of this logic is that the cause of burnout is rooted, most often, in working with traumatized or "troubled" recipients of care and that burnout is, thus, a kind of "compassion fatigue" or vicarious trauma—not necessarily complicated by the helper's own "troubles" or traumas.

Let me return, then, to thinking about whether or not "burnout" is the most accurate way to think about the kind of fatigue Raj describes, a fatigue that is deeply familiar to anyone who has been a "voluntary gender worker" for a significant amount of time. Historically, this kind of work is unpaid. We're only just beginning to inhabit, for better or worse, more formalized non-profit and institutional structures that variously—and unevenly—remunerate such labor, and the trans folks who inhabit these kinds of positions often come into them after years of unpaid hustle. Raj is a case in point, here—he got his credentials as a psychotherapist in 2001 and only then was able to make a living doing the kind of work he'd *already* been doing for decades, by finally legibly inserting himself within the diagnostic and treatment apparatus he'd worked for years to help build, particularly as the founder of the Foundation for the Advancement of Canadian Transsexuals (FACT, formed in 1978) and, for years, through his magazines, newsletters, consultations and trainings, and public advocacy. His experience of burnout occurs within the context of unwaged, "voluntary" labor, but what can "voluntary" possible mean in a context like the one Raj transitioned within, with no formal workplace protections, without a streamlined process to access technologies of transition or to modify gender documentation to make one's legal identity consistent, and with the constant risk of being outed in transphobic workplaces? It is not just a problem of long hours, emotionally extractive labor, underpayment, and underappreciation—though it is, of course, most of those things. It is experiencing all of this in the absence of wages and *having* to engage in this kind of unwaged labor to build an ever-so-slightly habitable world for trans folks. I'll let Raj tell it:

> In fact, my preoccupation with the welfare of the transgender community is the reason why today I am without a paying career or steady source of income. Don't get me wrong, this was my choice and mine alone (my mission or calling in life) to serve this neglected, misunderstood and, even today, stigmatized class of people—rare victims of what Kim Stuart has so aptly termed "the uninvited dilemma" [of gender dysphoria]. After all, I am a post-op F-M TS [female-to-male transsexual] myself and I guess I want to "take care of my own." (1987, 3)

When Raj dedicated himself to networking, organizing, and advocacy on the part of trans communities, he made a decision quite counter to the standard, hegemonic medical advice given to trans folks in the 1970s, which was to go stealth, blend in, and live as normatively as possible. This was a choice, yes, but certainly not an unconstrained one. When reality is so markedly discriminatory, the advice that one should go stealth and proceed with life as if the fact that one was trans were irrelevant radically underdetermines the extent to which being trans *continues to matter,* even "post" transition.

In a situation of unwaged affective labor as a "voluntary gender worker," what tools does one have to deal with burnout? There is no vacation time or "flextime" and often a scarce support network that could take over one's responsibilities while one takes time out for self-care and healing. In the nascent days of trans advocacy and activism, it is very possible—indeed, likely—that there was no one waiting in the wings to take on the forms of unwaged labor so necessary to securing access to transition-related procedures. Who was lining up to take the reins of *Metamorphosis* or *Gender NetWorker*? Who was ready and willing to step in and become the coordinator of FACT? Given the wide geographic dispersal and extensive closeting of trans folks in the 1970s and 1980s (testified to by the fact that so many communicated through a robust network of newsletters and periodicals, punctuated by the occasional regional meet-up if one was lucky enough to live in or adjacent to a metropole), who had the time, emotional bandwidth, and energy to do this kind of work? I imagine the list was quite short.

Being a "voluntary gender worker" means you are, as Raj says, taking care of your own. This is doubly so if you are experiencing the social death and natal alienation so common to trans experiences. The boundaries between who is a carer and who is a recipient of care are pretty radically blurred in such a situation; any act of caring is simultaneously an act of maintaining those minimal networks of support that sustain you. Trans collectives and communities are deeply interwoven and interdependent, enmeshed in a way that makes distinguishing between the roles of carer and recipient difficult—they're rotating, interchangeable, and reciprocal. Or, as that ubiquitous bumper sticker familiar to all caretakers of dogs would have it: it's hard to know, once and for all, "who's rescuing who."

The language of "compassion fatigue" or "vicarious trauma" becomes challenging here. Compassion—the experience of deep sorrow or sympathy for the suffering of an other—is an inadequate affective accounting of what transpires when a community or collective is involved in acts of caring and being cared for that are informed by similar and mutually resonating forms of traumatization. Other terms utilized within the psychological literature for this phenomenon are "secondary traumatization" or "secondary traumatic stress," which enumerate a hierarchy of traumatization that can't possibly, in its ordinal logic, do justice to the kinds of mutual traumatic resonance that circulate between trans subjects involved in acts of caring.

The framework offered by burnout posits a discrete subject or subjects as the source of the carer's fatigue, stress, and trauma. It encourages the person suffering burnout to causally transfer these allied negative affects to an other or others, who then become the source of the burnout that affects the subject. This denies the very basic facts of interdependency, mutuality, and subject interwovenness and encourages us to minimize the complexity of the affective interchanges at work when marginalized subjects engage in the work of making each other's lives more possible.

How can we think beyond burnout? How can we do justice to the fact that we are often triggered by one another in the act of caring but nevertheless *need* one another, in both specific and abstract ways, to get by?

## Three Billboards: Abstraction, Attention, Anonymity

In the summer of 2019, a billboard went up at the corner of Seven Mile and Kempa Street in Detroit; it read, simply, "Trans People Are Sacred." The text—black handwritten centered in the top third of the billboard—floats in white space above a series of brightly colored vertical rectangles, all with rounded corners. In the center of the piece is a dusty pink arch, its ends filled in with red and capped by a black stripe with white dots. As the gaze moves from left to right, the colors shift from jewel tones to a palette dominated by light blue and pink—the colors of the trans pride flag. The height of the rounded oblongs raises toward the margins of the billboard, and tapers down in the center. They might be built spaces that form an amorphous cityscape; they might be subjects grouped tightly and reduced to chromatic abstractions; some of these shapes might be phallic, but none are brutalist or hard-edged in their monumentality. They're gently amorphous, luminous, warm. If this is a cityscape, it is one that loves you back. If these shapes are loosely figured bodies, reduced to richly saturated auras, then this is a loving kind of minimalism that evades the economies of representation that do such violence to trans people.

It is no surprise to me that a billboard declaring the sacrality of trans existence deals in abstraction. In a context where demands on tokenized trans visibility are rife—where we are constantly being asked to show up and speak and act on behalf of our "community" (another abstraction, one that's sometimes useful and usually fallacious)—and where such visibility relentlessly and predictably exposes one to violence, it's a real relief to be hailed by a beautiful blob. Sometimes being trans feels like wanting to resist and evade spectacularized visibility with every fiber of your being; sometimes it feels like just wanting to be seen in all your banality, sleepily chomping on a banana while wearing sweatpants. Ever since *Trap Door* came out in 2018, the radical academics and cultural producers among us keep repeating the refrain that guides that book: visibility is a trap. We're just recycling Foucault and repurposing a quip of his from *Discipline and Punish*—the one where he's talking about Bentham and panopticism and he's like *y'all, to be seen is to be surveilled and to be surveilled is to be controlled and when you're so routinely surveilled you internalize that shit and surveil yourself constantly.*

The trans specificity to this has to do with the fact that we are clocked relentlessly, disproportionately surveilled and disproportionately prone to internalize such surveillance and self-surveil. When your body becomes a problem—and trans bodies are nothing if not problems, institutionally speaking—it also becomes the space where possible solutions get worked out, and this process can intensify anxieties around appearance. There is a ready and waiting medical industry that serves us in incredibly integral ways but that also makes us pay out of pocket for all sorts of procedures, even those of us who have purportedly trans-inclusive insurance, and all of these procedures aim to make us more passable, more cistypical, more reprotypical. So many trans guys with their anxieties about their height, the size of their hands and feet, anxieties that don't seem to go away no matter how much facial hair you grow or how small and well-healed your top surgery scars are. A friend of mine over dinner, last year, as we talked about hormone blockers and The Trans Youth: "it's wild to think that soon, there will be really tall trans guys, with big hands." And then, for trans women: electrolysis. Voice coaching. Facial feminization surgery. For those of us with reproductive organs that work the way they are expected to work: fertility preservation, gamete freezing, the questions of orchiectomy and hysterectomy, of whether or not to cycle off hormones in order to conceive.

The problem of the body feels endless because the situations wherein it becomes a problem often seem to just go on and on: discontinuous identity documentation, the ubiquity of gender markers, the dissonance produced by the friction between these markers and our modes of appearance, "groin anomalies" as we pass through the ProVision L3, being called out of a moment of blissful forgetfulness of our embodied selves by a street harasser or a misgendering coworker. The panopticon is real, and it is gendered, and we are constantly, constantly reminded of this.

For all these reasons, many trans folks resist, both implicitly and explicitly, what photographic theorist John Tagg calls the "burden of representation" (1993) and the institutional demands for transparency, legibility, and the determinacy and continuity of identity that come with it. Passing is a fragile art, dependent on, among many other variables, the light. Flood lights are transphobic. Hypervisibility and the drive to transparency, and the technologies that enable it, are not trans-friendly. I think micha cárdenas makes this point best, in a larger meditation on the role of technologies of visibility in the lives of trans folks of color:

> Passing is not simply a question of being or becoming visible or invisible, but instead a question of attaining a particular form of visibility. Often, for trans women of color, the question of passing can be determined by the amount of light and the color of light reflected from one's face and neck. This light can determine one's ability to survive or not, as in the case of Islan Nettles, a black trans woman who was murdered in New York after her catcaller decided that she was a trans woman. . . . Passing involves both the modulation of visibility by the person who is passing but also the reception of that image by the viewer who makes a decision about whether or not a person fits into a particular category. (2015)

Another friend of mine—a woman who made a career out of adventure sports photography and authoring guidebooks, who transitioned later in life, in a totally bro-dominated field, and has gone on to become one of the most visible trans advocates in the outdoor industry—has a quote from inspirational speaker Brené Brown tattooed on her forearm. It reads "show up and be seen." Which is brave and inspiring when you feel afraid to leave the house, worried about coming out to lovers and friends. But also, and equally important, is the practice of learning when and how to camouflage oneself, when and how to sidestep visibility, to not be seen or to be seen only fleetingly, flittingly, in order to evade identification, to avoid being clocked. To read the light as if it's a barometer of relative safety; to read the space and the bodies around you to gauge their potential hostility, their belligerent reactivity. This is true, too, if you're trying to maintain a grasp on some kind of optimism during your everyday perambulations—nothing throws you out of a good mood like the unchecked transphobia of a stranger. Modulations of visibility aren't always about life or death, but also, at some level, they *are*. How much shit can you metabolize and still be expected to keep on living, to keep on desiring this world?

There is also a strange anxiety induced by mainstream economies of trans representation, because most of the folks we *do* see are impeccably beautiful and deeply cis-passing trans women. Rarely do we see representations of folks in the midst of transition, trans guys with acne and cracked voices, whose sebaceous glands are going wild; bare-faced trans femmes who haven't yet shaved. We are flawed, imperfect, sometimes rough in our becomings. For me, this is a kind of beauty that trumps any seamless, airbrushed art of surfaces. But the folks who actively bless our mess are few and far between.

Because of all this, there is a comfort in abstraction. Curator Ashton Cooper, in a preface to a 2016 roundtable titled "Queer Abstraction," comments on how abstraction gets deployed "in the service of marginalized bodies to address problems of language and the complexity of subject formation in a binary world," how a plunge into indeterminacy makes us "step outside prevailing modes of understanding both selfhood and language" (2017, 286). This describes a transsexual mood, for sure. It names the linguistic and epistemological crisis we regularly produce and also a fantasy structure of reprieve where we might, for just a moment, leave that crisis behind.

Which is precisely how I feel when I see Jonah Welch's billboard. Anonymous, named but not represented, and hailed in the complexity of my need—to be seen and unseen simultaneously, to be comforted and also left alone, to, for once, feel held and witnessed within a public space without being made subject to other people's witness of me. But then again, this billboard lives ephemerally, in a particular neighborhood, in a specific city, in a perennially and irrevocably cracked world. The opening of a BuzzFeed article on the project recounts, "when nonbinary trans artist Jonah Welch went to check out their gorgeous new billboard in Detroit, someone drove by and yelled 'what the fuck' at them" (Strapagiel 2019). Trans antagonism persists, and so do we, in all our profanity, all our banality—and our sacredness, too.

A second billboard, this one near the border of Joshua Tree and Twentynine Palms, graces the Morongo Basin of the Mojave Desert with a message, white text on a black background, that reads

TRANSGENDER PEOPLE

DESERVE

HEALTH CARE ● SUPPORT

JUSTICE ● SAFETY ● LOVE

The text is surrounded by a banner frame, rendered in blue, yellow, green, brown, beige, and red interwoven stripes that look suspiciously akin to the palette and line work of trans artist Edie Fake, who is a resident of the Morongo Basin. While we can't attribute the board to him, we can maybe presume he helped render it. It was paid for by a group that calls themselves the Morongo Basin Neighbors, and it went up in the exact spot where a trans-baiting and trans-scapegoating political billboard used to be. In the lead-up to the 2016 election season, congressional candidate Tim Donnelly leased this big rectangle to excoriate his opponent, emblazoning it with the exhortation to "Ask Paul Cook Why He Voted To Allow Our Military Funds to Be Used for Sex-Change Surgeries!" Incumbent Cook had apparently voted, as recounted in the regional newspaper the *Hi-Desert Star,* "against a spending bill amendment that would have ended the Pentagon policy of providing gender-reassignment surgeries if a doctor deemed them medically necessary" (Moore 2018).

And so we move from undeserving citizen-subjects to people worthy of care, from frivolously gendered, deranged monsters on the outskirts of rights recognition draining the public coffers to a site of both lack and need. In this deeply schizoid political moment, these are the public roles available to us, altogether undeserving of care, on one side, and the demographic most in need of robust rights protection at both state and federal levels, on the other. This billboard swap is paradigmatic of the ways in which we enter into hegemonic political discourse in the current, radically bifurcated political moment—as wedge edge issue par excellence.

When the Morongo River Neighbors declare our deservingness, I'm reminded viscerally of all the shit dealt our way. I read "health care support justice safety love" as a litany of the things we currently lack, though surely, it can't be all slow death, homicide, suicide, and sustained institutional and interpersonal violence. I, at least, have and experience "health care support justice safety love" in some significant measure—in large part because of a combination of racial, educational, and recent economic privilege—although I remember lacking in many of these categories at some point or another, with some of these points very recent. Finding myself embedded in toxic dynamics because dysphoria and a history of abuse had me convinced I was trash, thus deserving of the trash certain folks dealt. Refusing to visit medical professionals for years, although I had some form of insurance for most of that time, because I was terribly afraid of how they would respond to this intersex, trans body. Feeling like I had to be extra high-performing in graduate school because the academy hadn't yet begun to cannibalize junior trans scholars, and I was convinced I couldn't get away with writing about any of the things I'm currently preoccupied with and still have a successful career. Intense anxiety in public spaces and a tendency to stay indoors or alone in the woods (I mean, I still have this anxiety and I still embrace my inner curmudgeonly hermit). And I'm brutally and continually aware that this history is akin and overlapping with the bios of so many other trans folks.

Strange to be triggered by a trans-positive billboard. Strange to be triggered by public gestures of inclusion and allyship.

I'm writing this in O'Hare Airport on a brilliant fall day, staring out the big plate glass windows that make the terrible architecture of airports moderately habitable because at least you can escape to a distant horizon line. I look at the faraway silhouette of the Chicago skyline and think about the woman that checked me in at the tiny airport in State College, Pennsylvania—my current home—this morning. Approaching the counter, she sunnily sang a name for me that started with "Mr." After scanning my ID, where my gender is marked "F," she changed her tune to "Ms." I told her that I don't use either of those honorifics, at which point she stepped out from behind the counter, scanned me up and down, and proceeded to tell me how "cool" she thought that was but also how perplexing that made things for her, who had to use such honorifics as part of the corporate protocol for customer engagement. "But," I thought, "you don't. You could simply just not, and the odds of anyone reporting you—especially the odds of visibly gender nonconforming folks reporting you—are basically nil." I didn't say that, though. Instead, feeling vulnerable and sleepy and loath to engage in this silver-platter teachable moment when I was just trying to make sure I got my frequent flyer miles added to this work trip, I invoked all of the occupational privilege I have and said, "Well, I'm a doctor, so you could just use that." She of course presumed that meant I was an MD.

What does it mean that folks so routinely internalize the injunction to perform such gendered forms of respectful solicitation by professional behest? That this kind of formalism trumps better sense, better relational intuition? Why couldn't she just *not*? Why has the problem become how to more effectively slot us into preexisting institutional logics? Why are even the most radically nonreformist among us still so often ventriloquizing a thin, accommodationist rhetoric of inclusion? While the more prominent nonprofits, both trans-specific and trans-adjacent, from the NCTE to Lambda Legal and the ACLU, have been taking up the question of trans rights, there is also a small chorus of activists and intellectuals advocating for gender abolition—from built space (fuck a single-sex bathroom) to identity markers (who needs an "X" when you can just leave the whole category off) to professional sports (why are folks still advocating binary sex verification testing when we know, and have always already known, that sex itself *is not binary*)?

What would gender be if we abolished it at institutional, legal, and juridical levels?

Could we have it without it having us?

Would we mourn it as a kind of loss?

Would we monumentalize its absence?

When I think about loss and gender, I think about another billboard: Felix Gonzalez-Torres's empty bed, with its two dented pillows and its rumpled sheets and its grayscale and its size, bigger than any bed I've slept in but not yet big enough to hold our grief. A visual parable for the AIDS epidemic, for the loss of lovers and the disruption of intimacies and the loneliness and the fear of aloneness. But also, all of the love we lose by virtue of being who we are, the abandonments, the cold beds, the lovers left and leaving who couldn't see us correctly, who we could not adapt to, who could not adapt to us, whose desires diverged along the gendered lines we were insistent on crossing. This emptiness not just a parable but also a preamble, an opening into another form of life.

There are genders and there is Gender and I believe we can have the former without the latter. We can refuse and dismantle the structuring logic and inhabit its ruins resistantly—to be femme is nothing if it isn't this. Some of us do and don't survive. There are many empty beds, many missing persons, many mourned bodies. We can lose and gain genders on our way to losing Gender.

T Fleischmann, in *Time is the Thing a Body Moves Through*, writes about doing an art project with a friend in the woods of

Tennessee, outside a cabin at one of the handful of queer communes in East Tennessee. They pulled out a big mirror and put it on a couple of workhorses and dumped out all their pills (hormones, AIDS meds) and spelled out "POST-SCARCITY." They took photos of it, with the mirror reflecting a bluebird sky.

They did this in a moment of estrogen shortage throughout the United States, in a moment where former hedge-fund manager and CEO of Turing Pharmaceuticals raised the price of an AIDS-related medication (Daraprim, which is routinely prescribed to folks with weakened immune systems in order to treat toxoplasmosis) from $13.50 a pill to $750. The medications we rely upon to stay alive seemed to be becoming rapidly unavailable, though they were already deeply inaccessible to many—who lacked insurance, had no access to physicians, or stayed away from medical establishments out of fear of maltreatment. A postscarcity vision guides this ongoing moment where, increasingly, folks are sharing hormones, subsidizing each other's medical care, crowdsourcing money for rent, for transition, for bail. In situations of ever-tightening austerity, dispossession, and deprivation, we cultivate methods of collective survival that aren't just guided by an imaginary of abundance but bring such abundance to bear in the present. Which brings me back to care.

# Theorizing Trans Care

## Assembled with Care

Assemblage thinking comes easily to trans folks. Most of us find Eurocentric myths of maximal agency, atomistic selfhood, and radical self-possession a really hard sell. We lack the privilege of having an uncomplicated "I" (and the ability to conjure oneself into such an "I" is always a product of privilege, to be sure). Recognition comes to us in the form of a gift—though we tell others what pronouns to use, what names, how to refer to us, we're also thrown directly into a series of complicated ratiocinations as we attempt to infer how others are *understanding* their conferral of gender unto us. In a 2019 interview following the publication of Andrea Long Chu's *Females,* she and McKenzie Wark directly address this:

> **MW:** The way I read it, the way you're thinking about gender, is that it's always in the gift of the other. It's not "mine." I rely on the gift of the other to have it at all. But then that implies an ethics. Right? Is that a way to connect these two things—language and gender—together?
>
> **ALC:** Do you mean that it implies an ethics in the sense that you are also giving gender to other people?
>
> **MW:** Yes. Both being indebted to the other and giving it to others. But I think if you start, first, with just the dyad, a me and a

you, then one starts as a supplicant, requiring that the other give gender back to me. And for us, for trans people, it's in the way we are asking; in that, for us to be free to be ourselves is to insist that others give recognition to our gender.

**ALC:** Right. Yeah. The thing that I am especially thinking about when I say something like that about gender, on the most granular empirical level, is early transition. For instance: I was out at NYU, I was in New York. I was surrounded by people who were more or less prepared to give me what I was asking for, right? So in a sense there was, on a sort of surface level, there was a kind of generosity there. And then I would go into Walgreens or whatever, and have an interaction with someone at the register, and get misgendered, and would instinctively consider that a more genuine reaction than the reaction of people in my department or friends of mine. And, in part, that's because the cashier was probably telling me something that felt like it had the structure of something like a secret. And so it felt realer. But it was also because actually that person owed me nothing.

**MW:** Right. So that's an honest statement from the cashier.

**ALC:** The person at Walgreens had the opportunity to actually be genuinely generous, which is to say, to know nothing about me. The problem with my friends is that they were my friends.

I love Wark's phraseology in this passage, love her articulation of supplication as the existential posture of gender. One asks for it, one relies on the other to grant it, to confer the desired recognition. We may attempt to exert some minimal agency as supplicants—semaphore certain visual, auditory, and linguistic cues—but we are in no way in control of the exchange, can in no way determine the outcome. In relationships structured by mutual indebtedness or reciprocal duty—where we know and thus owe the other—we usually get what we want, insofar as gendered recognition is concerned. It's still a process of supplication, but in friendship, we're bossy bottoms—and our friends are, usually, service tops.

But the encounter with the stranger has always held the real weight—and burden—as far as the conferral of gender goes.

As Chu says, it feels "realer." This is, of course, why "real-life tests"—where folks were expected to live in their gender full-time *before* being given access to surgery and, sometimes, hormones as well—were given such weight in the early decades of medical transition. Though the gatekeeping and the emphasis on cisnormative, heterosexual desirability (not to mention the ways in which both of these expectations were shaped implicitly by White aesthetic ideals and gendered norms) was (and remains, when and where it operates) ethically and politically abhorrent, there is a certain operative truth that subtends the practice: that social recognition, and nothing other than social recognition, grounds gender. It is from such social recognition that assumptions regarding embodiment (and, particularly, genital configuration) are made. This is what Talia Mae Bettcher is getting at when she writes about the ways in which gender presentation "isn't merely a euphemism for restricted discourse about genitalia, it's a euphemistic stand-in for genitals" (2012, 329). She details how, in Eurocentered cultures, the boundaries that regulate intimacy (through degrees of proximity and distance) implicitly denote who has access to the body parts deemed "intimate." The most "intimate" of these parts—the genitals—are also subject to a differentially and dichotomously gendered moral structure, where (so-called) male genitals are presumed to be "violating" and (so-called) female genitals are "violated" or violatable (326). This then entails differential motivation for practices of clothing-as-concealment: "a female will cover up to protect her privacy, whereas a male will cover up to prevent his body from offending through indecency" (327).

The crux of Bettcher's argument is this: there is a whole moral structure that frames and regulates intimacy that gender presentation *stands in for* when it's understood according to a "natural attitude" (Bettcher 2012, 319) that infers genitalia from gender presentation. When we talk about forms of gendered recognition feeling "realer" or less real, my hunch is that the most "real" moments of recognition are those wherein we slip seamlessly into this moral structure. What jars about trans modes of gender presentation that aren't stealth is that they disrupt the moral order that regulates intimacy (and that, thus, constitutes the public/private divide). This is why trans subjects are so often asked questions that euphemize about genital status: questions about having had "the surgery" or being "really" men or women. Our rebuttal to these questions is that they're *indecent*, that they reference intimate matters that shouldn't be routinely parsed in the public realm, that they're questions that have no place in a public sphere where moral belonging hinges on genital concealment, in a moral order where the only people who need or get to know the answer are those with whom we're *intimate*.

We come to gender as supplicants, all of us. And many of us fail the litmus test of decency because our modes of gender presentation are too vulgar, too louche, or genderfucked in such a way that we disrupt the "natural attitude" because we fail to enact and achieve a certain verisimilitude of normative, White maleness or femaleness. Failing this litmus test means we are repeatedly refused, turned away in moments of our imploring recognition. I'd wager that all trans people carry within them the memory of such refusals, even if they no longer actively shape our everyday engagements. This means that we all recognize gender as a morally loaded laborious *process*. It is *work*. And our labor is alienated, insofar as we don't own what we produce and we rely on someone else to determine its value and worth.

This means that we labor under conditions we don't choose, conditions that many of us actively want to destroy. But we also understand, intimately, that the concept of autonomy that underwrites romantic myths of the insurrectionary subject can't hold. Gender recognition is sustained by a web of forces that we don't control. Because we rely on others for recognition, we understand how selfhood is given through such forms of recognition. Because, when such recognition is withheld, we intimately sense that we are being relegated to the position of the monstrous, simultaneously both more and less than human. Because we exert agency in determining our forms of life and flesh, but that agency is always only one part of a much broader assembly into which our flesh—and its possibilities—are grafted.

Trans studies, as a field, has tended to approach the relation between trans experience and assemblage thinking through a focus on how our bodies are naturalcultural entities engaged (in a variety of heteroclite, divergent ways) in projects of bio-technical alteration. Not surprisingly, the emphasis has come to fall on the interface of trans embodiment with the medical-industrial complex, and articulations of trans-embodiment-as-assemblage have focused intensively on this nexus. What gets overlooked in this scholarship—my own on the topic included—are the ways in which everyday acts of interpersonal recognition are the crucible through which such assemblages come into (il)legibility. From Susan Stryker's "My Words to Victor Frankenstein above the Village of Chamonix" (1992) to Karen Barad's "TransMaterialities: Trans*/Matter/Realities and Queer Political Imaginings" (2015), trans bodies as particular-ly *Frankensteinian*—and thus naturalcultural assemblages par excellence—has dominated, though many of us are quick to point out that what is true of trans bodies is not at all particular to them—indeed, normatively gendered cis people, too, are just as assembled, just as biotechnically mediated, as we are. The deployment of the trans-body-as-assemblage, in its circuitous and widespread reiterations, bears a certain pedagogical and ontological value, as it demonstrates the stitched-together, intra-active constitution of *all* embodiment. Building upon Stryker's call for cis folks "to investigate [their] nature" as she has been compelled to (1994, 241), Barad writes that "materiality in its entangled psychic and physical manifestations is always already a patchwork, a suturing of disparate parts" (2015, 393).

So, while trans bodies are routinely theorized as a prompt for cis folks to reconsider the "nature of nature" (Barad 2015, 392) and, by extension, the nature of embodiment, we have not thought very much, or very carefully, about whether and what form of an ethics might spring from such a reconsideration. In other words, it matters deeply both *how* we care and *who* cares for these assemblages we are. Wark, Bettcher, and Chu each, in their way, point toward the fact that there is indeed, whether or not we like or desire it, a hierarchy of verisimilitude that continues to reign in the majority of our social interactions. This hierarchy determines, to a large extent, both whether and how we are understood as belonging to collectivities and communities. It plays a significant role in the frequency, intensity, and forms of violence to which we are or are not exposed. It plays out on the most mundane levels and mitigates our possibilities for agency, autonomy, and action—in other words, it informs how and where we may assemble our bodies and selves in interaction. When we show up in public, when we plug our assembled bodies into an assembled public, what's the ethos?

**Transing Care**

When I invoke the question of ethos, I'm calling attention to collective ways of doing and the norms and principles that emerge from such ways of doing. This is a very different conception of ethical behavior than one that proceeds from ethical rules or first principles and features a moral agent who has maximal agency and unmitigated choice in the actions they take. An ethos emerges from an ensemble of practices; when we shift collective practice, we reconfigure ethos. Practices of care are always part of an emergent ethos. Because care isn't abstract, but only ever manifested through practice—action, labor, work—it is integral to our ways of doing.

In thinking through the relation of ethos and care, I'm following the work of María Puig de la Bellacasa, who writes that ethical obligations of care are "commitments that stabilize as necessary to maintain or intervene in a particular ethos (agencies and behaviors within an ecology). They are not a priori universal, they do not define a moral, or social, or even natural 'nature': they *become* necessary to the maintaining and flourishing of a relation through processes of ongoing relating" (2017, 154). So much of contemporary trans activism is about intervening in a particular ethos (that is trans-exclusionary or trans-antagonistic) in order to shift relational terrain in ways that are more inclusive. Think, at the level of pedagogy, of the innovations deployed in classrooms—pronoun go-rounds, slots for chosen names on index cards, use of the singular "they" in course materials, the list goes on and on. At the level of institutions: shifts in bathroom architecture, calls for implicit bias trainings, enabling the digital systems utilized to facilitate name and gender-marker changes without flagging security threats. At the level of the juridical: bringing cases against insurance exclusions for trans-related procedures, ensuring that trans folks are able to readily and easily navigate the bureaucracies that determine access to name and gender-marker changes. None of these struggles are particularly sexy, and it's easy to indict any of them as accommodationist and reformist. Yet they are each necessary, and cumulatively they lay the groundwork that begins to ensure that basic access to public space is possible for trans subjects. This work—like all care work—is about fostering survival; it is maintenance work that must be done so that trans folks can get about the work of living. But the mere necessity of this work also points to the fact that the most fundamental networks of care that enable us to persist in our existence are often threadbare or, sometimes, nearly nonexistent.

In the summer of 2019, Aren Aizura and I cotaught an intensive course on trans and queer care labor. In drafting our rationale for the course, we were forced to grapple with the failure of dominant articulations of care work and care ethics to do justice to the complexities of care labor trans subjects both need and undertake. We wrote about how feminist theorists of care have yet to substantively address queer and trans forms of care labor, instead centering women's domestic labor within heteronormative households, naturalizing a set of values from such labor, then extrapolating and exploring the deprioritization of those values in the public sphere (Berg 2014). Domestic and transnational feminist examinations of care labor, relatedly, rely on a logic that undergirds theories of the relations of gender and care labor, which Martin Manalansan frames as "domestic = family = heterosexual woman = care and love" (2008).

We wanted to think about what care labor and ethics looks like if we start from a different set of locations and relations. We tried to begin not with the family but instead from the intricately interconnected spaces and places where trans and queer care labor occurs: the street, the club, the bar, the clinic, the community center, the classroom, the nonprofit, and sometimes, yes, the home—but a home that is often a site of rejection, shunning, abuse, and discomfort. We asked:

> What happens if we decenter the emphasis on the domestic and the reproductive that has so long informed theorizations of care, and begin instead by investigating networks of mutual aid and emotional support developed by trans femme communities subject to transmisogyny, transmisogynoir, and multiple, interlocking forms of institutional marginalization and structural violence? Or when we investigate caretaking labor involved in forms of historical recovery that piece together trans and queer

intergenerational memory and knowledge production in the face of mechanisms of elision, erasure, and absence? (Aizura and Malatino 2019)

The terrain of what constitutes care shifts radically once such decentering occurs. For queer and trans subjects, this is often less about exporting the feminized values of care associated with the White, bourgeois home to the public sphere than it is about seeking ways to make the multivalent and necessary care hustle that structures so many of our lives more sustainable, especially as we're often actively engaged in inventing or piecing together the units—domestic, familial, intimate—that are just assumed a priori in much literature on care labor and care ethics.

So how do we do that? Through mutual aid, which Dean Spade glosses as "work that directly addresses the conditions the movement seeks to address, such as by providing housing, food, health care, or transportation in a way that draws attention to the politics creating need and vulnerability" (Spade 2019). Through what Aizura calls the "communization of care" (2017)—which is a practice of reworking care so that it doesn't rely on the family, one's intimate circle, or an abstraction of community as its locus of distribution and circulation but instead organizes care around those with whom we are socially consubstantial (Povinelli 2008, 511), all those folks with whom we're interdependent, many of whom we may not know intimately or at all. Through what I've called an "infrapolitical ethics of care" (Malatino 2019), which indexes the forms of care that enable co-constituted, interdependent subjects to repair, rebuild, and cultivate resilience in the midst of, and in the aftermath of, experiences of overwhelming negative affect. Through drawing on what Amy Marvin calls "trans ethical wisdom" about communal "solidarity in dependency" (Marvin 2019, 112), where she focuses on the mutual caregiving enacted by trans women of color Sylvia Rivera and Marsha

P. Johnson through their work with STAR (Street Transvestite Action Revolutionaries) House, where they practically fostered the survival of trans youth and street queens expelled from most all hegemonic loci of care. And, finally, though not exhaustively, through what I've described as a "t4t [trans4trans] praxis of love," which is many things: "an ideal, a promise, an identifier, a way of flagging an ethic of being. It is antiutopian, guiding a praxis of solidarity in the interregnum; it is about small acts guided by a commitment to trans love, small acts that make life more livable in and through difficult circumstances" (Malatino 2019). These concepts all overlap, and we can shift between them as we recalibrate and continue to develop an ethic of care that ensures trans survival and flourishing in the midst of ongoing racialized depredation, rampant and metastasizing economic inequality, and imminent environmental collapse.

## Mismeasuring Care

Though care is fundamental to our continued survival and flourishing, it is impossible to calculate within a logic of exchange, though we seem to try our damnedest. The main insights of Marxist feminism bear precisely on the simultaneous necessity and incalculability of care, insofar as it argues that though reproductive labor is labor is considered beyond, adjacent to, or on the margins of the market, it is nevertheless labor without which the market—and our collective selves—would collapse. What the wages for housework demand (Dalla Costa and James 1975) illuminates is the fundamental necessity of reproductive labor. If minoritized, feminized, and racialized brown and Black subjects failed to perform it, the economic system would rapidly become inoperative.

Care work is essential, though historically and contemporaneously either unremunerated or very poorly remunerated. Care work is work, but a form of work that is consistently denied and disavowed. Whatever the economic form of social organization we happen to inhabit, whatever the locale, whatever the historical moment, care work is necessary for survival and flourishing. We are fundamentally dependent and thus fundamentally interdependent. The work we do to keep each other alive exceeds mensuration. How could we ever actually quantify the daily acts of care that circulate in the interspecies milieu we inhabit? I think of something simple—a squabble with my long-term partner about whose turn it is to do the dishes. This quickly devolves into a mutual, tit-for-tat list-off concerning our domestic labor ("Well, I took the dogs out this morning," "Well, I shoveled the driveway yesterday," "Well, I changed the cat litter today," on and on). We stop after a minute and laugh, hard, realizing the obvious fact that both of us, intimately entwined in our domesticity, are doing essential work according to our relative and fluctuating capacities and that this work is actively aiding the flourishing of the other. Keeping count is futile and unnecessary; the rhythms of our care work are tied to the frailty or strength of our bodies, our fluctuating levels of exhaustion, the intensity of the demands placed on our time by other intimates, by our jobs, by advocacy work, by other dearly held commitments. The fantasy that care work—within and beyond the home—can be somehow equalized (a fantasy held dear by many feminists, myself included) ushers into the ostensible private sphere the same forms of neoliberal task tabulation that circulate (unjustly) in our waged labor. Why would we want that kind of accounting infecting our homeplaces? Why would we want to import it to those other spaces—of friendship, collectivity, community, solidarity—that we co-constitute and on which we depend? Why would we want to subject these relationships to the neoliberal "discourses around measuring, accounting, and auditing that have proliferated in management practices and institutional policies" (Manalansan 2018, 493)? But, more to the point, why does this tendency toward mensuration persist, even though we might understand that the care we perform and receive always takes place in excess of exchange logic?

If we're serious about addressing the production of burnout, fatigue, exhaustion, debility, and disability within trans lives and communities, we cannot afford to internalize and operationalize a concept of care as debt. As queer materialist feminist artists Park McArthur and Constantina Zavitsanos put it, "can we find other convivial forms for this labor (care work) that do not depend on exchange" (2013, 127)? And, once we do, "how are we to accept and coordinate our mutual and divergent forms of precarity and risk" as we go about such work (127)?

# Something Other Than
# Trancestors: Hirstory Lessons

### Insulation

In the summer of 2019, I started a new journaling practice. I was inspired by Lynda Barry, the cartoonist and novelist who, in 2011, began teaching a course called What It Is at the University of Wisconsin–Madison. That course sought to answer the following question: "If the thing we call 'the arts' has a biological function, what is it?"

The core of her exploration into what she calls the "unthinkable mind" (2014, 51)—more colloquially known as the unconscious—is a daily writing and drawing exercise meant to activate and access the unthought, to bring out some of its contents and translate them to the page. In this exercise, you divide a page into four uneven quadrants by drawing an upside down cross. In the top-left quadrant, you make a list of the things you did that day. In the top-right, a list of what you saw. On the bottom left, a shred of conversation you overheard. And on the bottom right, you draw—in thirty seconds or less—a sketch of something you saw.

I quickly became a devotee of this practice, but one element of it gave me persistent trouble. This surprised me, given that the exercise was predicated on instant, ostensibly noneffortful recall, a simple bubbling-up to the surface of consciousness of experiential fragments from one's day. I wasn't supposed to have to try. But every day, reliably, when I got to that third quadrant where I had to write down something I overheard, *I could not recollect anything.*

I pride myself on being a good listener. I prefer one-on-one conversations with friends and lovers. I spend a fair amount of my day-to-day life in relatively intense conversations, given that I'm a professor of gender and sexuality studies with a de-centered, fundamentally dialogic pedagogical practice. I do my best to stay sensitive and attuned to linguistic nuance, in speech and in writing. So why is it that, try as I might, I could not recall a single snippet of overheard conversation? Where was the disconnect happening?

Then a realization struck. This was about *gender.* And by that, I mean it was about *transness,* about gender nonconformance, ambiguity, and performative instability. From a very young age, I'd been subject to the speculative hypothesizing of strangers regarding gender. My high school bully, in a brutal iteration of this sort of transphobic speculation, once trailed me through a high school hallway demanding to—in his words—see my pussy. He wanted proof that I was a girl. My body, undergoing its uniquely intersex puberty, was manifesting in pretty masculine ways— facial hair, deepening voice—but I continued to dress tomboy-lite, shrouding my never-really-feminine body in baggy clothing. This wasn't the first time I'd been exposed to such a demand, but it was the most invasive yet. That would change, though. I lived, throughout my teens and twenties, with an omnipresent worry that when and where I appeared in public, I would be subject to stares and extemporaneous speechifying about my gender. I often—sometimes paranoically, perhaps—was convinced I heard whispering in my wake about whether I was a boy or a girl. I refused to stop going out, however—that wouldn't have been possible or tenable for me; I'm constitutionally antiagoraphobic. But what I did do—without ever admitting it to myself, without ever directly or intentionally trying—was develop the ability to *completely tune out* the conversations of strangers. I had culti-vated an intense inability to eavesdrop, and I didn't even realize I'd done so for . . . maybe decades? Until Lynda Barry prompted me to sit down, shut up, and think about what I'd overheard that day, and I—ever a student that aims to please—completely failed the exercise.

For days, I walked around attempting to tune into the conver-sations of others, trying desperately to bring my auditory sense-relation to the world into a more robust existence. It was really, really hard work; the strength of the habit I'd built was immense and recalcitrant. I had stonewalled the world's chatter, and I had to disassemble this wall brick by brick if I was going to cultivate an openness to the words around me. But this opening, like all openings, also intensified my sense of vulnerability, increased the likelihood of becoming wounded by some offhanded scrap of commentary.

When I told friends about this strange ability to turn the vol-ume on the world way, way down, some of them—all cis and relatively gender-normative—responded with envy. How conve-nient it must be, they said, thinking of all the times they'd become annoyed and exasperated with things they'd overheard: MAGA flunkies in the supermarket checkout line, caretakers desperately trying to cajole a child into silence, tech bros talking investment schemes at the airport. For them, this chatter is *noise*—a distrac-tion, not at all central to their day, their goals, their well-being. For me, the inability to hear this noise had become an index of exclusion and marginality. I had tuned out in order to pro-tect myself. The degree to which I was able to tune back in was the degree to which I felt at ease in a given social world. They

49

thought I had cultivated a superpower that enabled me to focus on whatever I deemed the most important task at hand; I knew that it was symptomatic of a larger propensity to recede from spaces I didn't feel I could trust.

I began to think seriously about the different ways that trans subjects cultivate detachment, distance, and numbness in order to survive in and through inuring ourselves to the hostilities that surround us. How many of us have had to devise strategies for withdrawal and escape? How often do we strategically muffle our sensorium to *get through* a situation? We've seen the statistics on trans subjects and substance abuse (and if you haven't, the gloss from the 2011 comprehensive survey on trans discrimination in the U.S. reads "26% use or have used alcohol and drugs to cope with the impacts of discrimination" [Grant et al. 2011, 81]). We know anecdotally that depression and anxiety are common, and the 2015 U.S. Trans Survey gave us numbers to back it up, reporting that "thirty-nine percent (39%) of respondents reported currently experiencing serious psychological distress, which is nearly eight times the rate reported in the U.S. population (5%)" (James et al. 2016, 105). Enough of the bleak statistics, though. If you're trans and of a certain age, you're already thoroughly schooled in the saturation of negative affect, the cultivation, manipulation, and mutation of our coping mechanisms, and the cumulative toll both of these things—inextricable, indissoluble—exert.

We do what we need to do to keep going.

For me that meant tuning the whole world out. The folks that are closest to me now are the ones that knew how to cut through that silence. This means that caring for us—and our practice of caring for one another—is no simple task; we're sometimes swaddled thick in completely justified defenses. We might not be able to hear you, or each other, very well at all.

## "I Am in Training, Don't Kiss Me"

Around the time I started insulating myself from my everyday surround, I became increasingly interested in trans, intersex, and queer archives. In retrospect, my decision to pursue archivally grounded research during my dissertation (and for years afterward) is intimately linked to the forms of social dissociation I had unintentionally embraced for the purposes of survival. When the milieu you inhabit feels hostile, it's deeply comforting to turn to text and image from another time. I was desperate for representation, but more than that, I was desperate for some sense that other subjects had encountered and survived some of the transphobic, cissexist bullshit with which I was being repeatedly confronted. I needed resources for resilience. I wanted a roadmap for another way of being.

It's during this time that I encountered Claude Cahun's work and, in particular, a photograph that I've been obsessed with for years. It's the one of Cahun with two dark dots over their nipples, in boxing gear, barbell on their lap, wearing a leotard that reads "I AM IN TRAINING DON'T KISS ME." The standard feminist analysis of the piece circulates around the gender transitivity of the image—is Cahun training to become, or unbecome, a woman? The flurry of postmodern academic criticism addressing Cahun's work tends to "focus on her identity, attempting to piece together a psychogram of the artist through her writings and photos to determine whether she felt at ease with her biologically assigned gender" (Wampole 2013, 103). All of this speculation about the intent of Cahun's work and what it might say about their gender identity. Most of it bores me. It seems obvious that Cahun is engaging in what we now understand as a trans aesthetic practice, and I don't think that claiming this is anachronistic or recuperative. I'm not interested in whether Cahun is "really" a lesbian,

"really" trans, "really" whatever, but what I am very, very interested in are the links that they build between transition, gender
instability, and desire.

Their pose is serving deep trans twink. The flattened chest, the
coquettish cock of the head, the handlebar mustache displaced
and inverted into smoothly pomaded spit curls, the training
motif—it is all very "daddy, teach me." This is, of course, absurdly
heightened by the textual declaration on the leotard, warning off
all potential suitors, highlighting the fragility of nascent sexuality, and calling attention to the way that countenancing another's
desire runs the risk of despoiling whatever form of gendered
sexuality is emerging here. The famed ambiguity of the photo
renders Cahun a kind of universally fungible object of desire—
maybe a boy, maybe a girl, maybe a man, maybe a woman, but
precisely none of these things. Whatever it is that you're into,
maybe they can become it—maybe they're in training to be the
whatever of your dreams.

This space—nascent, indeterminate, delivering an evasive image prone to the projections of others—resonates as a particularly
trans look. Inhabiting a gender-liminal or provisionally gendered
body—as so many of us do, before, during, or after "transition,"
whatever that is—means being subject to continuous erotic in-
terrogation, being tossed squarely onto the shores of cis shame
about their own desires, being made an impossible—and impos-
sibly disruptive—object of desire. There's a bright filament that
connects Cahun to Lou Sullivan, a gay trans man who wanted
nothing more than to be a hot "youngman" (a turn of phrase he
takes from John Rechy) who is voraciously desired by other men,
who nevertheless kept ending up with dudes who were deeply
uncomfortable with their own queer desires, who relentlessly
feminized him and refused to accept his masculinity unmitigated. His lover of the mid-1980s, referred to in the journals as T,
gets upset with him about not shaving: "He was complaining as

we were having sex that my whiskers were 'rubbing' him and he *hates* that. I asked 'What's the big deal? Yours rub me too.' He said 'I don't like having sex with men'" (Sullivan 2019, 308). This echoes the laments of his lovers from years prior, like J, of whom Lou writes: "There's a deal where they say some people want a girl with a penis so they get a girlish boy. Maybe J wants a boy with a vagina so he takes me, a boyish girl. I don't know. The whole deal's screwed up" (66).

The whole deal is screwed up. We're surrounded by faithless witnesses and fetishized by them to boot. Our bodies are inter-pellated as not enough, too much, but also—as Cahun's image makes vivid—desired and desirable precisely because of this, in ways that run roughshod over our gender identities, our sense of self. To kiss—to engage viscerally and intimately—might be to trigger, to run headlong into haptic and verbal forms of bodi-ly misrecognition. Desire and dysphoria are tightly bonded to one another, and in the midst of transition, even the most well-intentioned and routine forms of intimacy run the risk of being received as confirmation that an other wants a bodymind that we aren't (entirely or quite). These misrecognitions imprint us; they leave a psychic trace, one that often manifests as acute anx-iety about how we're being seen, how we're being interpellated, especially in moments of intense vulnerability.

Morty Diamond, in his short introduction to the edited vol-ume *Trans/Love: Radical Sex, Love, and Relationships beyond the Gender Binary,* speaks directly to this erotic anxiety when he writes of how, "as familial, social, and personal changes abound during transition, a question arises early: *Who is going to date me now*? Or if currently partnered, *Will my relationship survive this transition*?" (2011, 7). Cahun deflects this anxiety by holding a mirror up to the viewer that acknowledges their desire, and Cahun's desirability, but withholds engagement because of how such desire discomfitingly overcodes trans and genderqueer embodiments. Christy Wampole, in a beautiful essay on Cahun's work, describes their gaze as "impudent" (2013, 101)—that is, without shame. Refusing shame. This is part of the queerness of Cahun's work, obviously—to reject shame is to reject the main affect that structures hegemonic heterocisnormative and misogynist understandings of queer and femme sexuality. Cahun, instead, forces the viewer to grapple with their own crisis of meaning about attraction to nonbinary bodies. It's not their problem. They're busy becoming otherwise.

Cahun's work—and so many other archival traces of trans, intersex, and gender nonconforming lives—feels like a gift that I'm still figuring out how to use. All I know for sure is that it sparks a sense of connection that resonates even as it remains opaque. It makes me feel some kind of way: less alone. This doesn't mean I identify with Cahun, and it especially doesn't mean they grant me some sort of prototrans legacy. Jules Gill-Peterson, in her own meditation on the affective resonance of trans archives, explains this feeling perfectly, writing of an archival encounter that moved her to tears: "it wasn't a moment of clean identification with the past . . . the proximities of the archive disperse the feeling of otherwise being consumed by the present and its many emergencies—of living overexposed, on the other side of that so-called 'trans tipping point'" (2019). It's not *your* past to claim, but it still somehow slant rhymes with your present, this instance of trans worlding that happened long before we came to speak casually of a gender spectrum.

## The Spectrum and the Spectral

Pedagogically, I have become used to periodizing the emergence of the "gender spectrum" as a heuristic for understanding a postbinary proliferation of genders. When I teach it—usually in an intro course—the lesson goes something like this: In the 1950s,

54

sexologist John Money used gender (distinct from biological sex) as one of several variables for medical professionals to take into account in cases of intersex births, and it appeared as part of a list alongside items like hormonal sex, assigned sex, and chromosomal sex. Gender (or, as he put it in the mid-1950s, "gender identity/role") encompassed "all those things that a person says or does to disclose himself as having the status of a boy or man, girl or woman respectively. It includes, but is not restricted to, sexuality in the sense of eroticism" (Money, Hampson, and Hampson 1955, 310). This understanding of gender was then deployed within mid-twentieth century university-run gender identity clinics in the United States in order to diagnose and treat both intersex and trans individuals. In the late 1960s and 1970s, it was increasingly taken up by feminist theorists to think through the socially and culturally constructed dimensions of masculinity and femininity. Finally, in the 1990s and early aughts, we have the emergence of the gender spectrum, oriented by two deeply familiar poles, with a proliferation of gender identities and spectrums sandwiched between. Commence a proliferation of increasingly complex infographics: some are overlapping Venn diagrams, others with additional spectra beyond gender—spectra of biological sex and sexual orientation, for instance. Sometimes gender is differentiated into spectra of expression and spectra of identity. Sometimes the infographic takes the form of a chart with two axes, male and female, and an abundance of quadrants arrayed betwixt. Whatever visualization we prefer, we've become culturally quite familiar with the proliferative logic of the spectrum, and—as per my intro-level historical narrative—tend to periodize it as emerging within the last twenty or so years.

Predictably, each time I teach a class where this comes up, I leave feeling frustrated and bereft. I will never argue against the importance of articulating gender identity and will always gladly furnish whatever resources I'm aware of for doing so to my students. But frustration persists, because whenever I articulate the spectrum, I brush up against the ineffable. The account I give tracks an emergent model, a specific and historically circumscribed calculus for diagnosing, identifying, translating, and rendering legible the gorgeous messiness of trans, intersex, nonbinary, and otherwise gender nonconforming lives. The identities we claim, no matter how complex our list of modifiers, always seem to say both much more and much less than I'd like. Years of dwelling in trans archives—both digitally and in brick-and-mortar collections—have brought me headlong into this messiness, into the history of terminological debates (between transvestites and transsexuals, "TVs" and "TSs," between transsexual and transgender, between intersex and trans, between hermaphroditisms of the body and hermaphroditisms of the soul, I could go on and on) and their inevitable failure to do justice to the lives they purport to label and thus, in a way, bear witness to.

I've come into contact with so much ephemera, so many traces of a number of minor lives—not famous or infamous historical personages, but everyday trans folk. Those who sent their self-portrait in to a transvestite newsletter, who were anonymized in medical case studies, who wrote heartbreaking letters to doctors seeking transition-related services. I've been consistently confronted with an ethical dilemma, which is also an ethical injunction: How to do justice to these lives? How to write about them—on behalf of them, with them, for them, in memoriam of them? The language I use in an attempt to render them never seems to suffice. The problem might actually be one of language itself—diagnostic language, in particular, but not only. Roland Barthes wrote of what he called "the 'fascism' of language" (2002, 42). With this turn of phrase, he named what I find so consistently and profoundly troubling when writing about (of, for, with) those subjects who appear, spectral, in the archives: the fact that the categories operative in language—masculine/

feminine, or the informal, singular *you* and the formal, plural *you,* for instance—"are coercive laws" (42) that "permit communication . . . but in exchange (or on the other hand) impose a way of being, a subjecthood, a subjectivity on one: under the weight of syntax, one must be *this* very subject and not another" (41). Working with fragments, attempting to render them legible, to place them within broader narratives of trans hirstories, places you squarely in the center of this quandary. In order to communicate *about* these lives, you engage in forms of speculation, projection, invention, and translation that inevitably fail to render subjecthood faithfully. The piecemeal, the partial, the imperfect is all you have. Each claim you make is overdetermined and only ever *possibly* resonant with the vicissitudes of their lived experience. The terms you use to describe folks are inevitably, as Barthes attests, coercive, too forceful, assertive, and declarative to do justice to the complexity and nuance of experience. This intensifies with trans subjects, because we experience ourselves so often, and so acutely, as trapped and constrained by language.

I'm haunted by these archival specters, and by my sense of duty to them. Because, in some small way, by existing—however minimally or maximally, however "part-time" or "full-time" they were—they have made our existence possible. Because our lives are, in some opaque and difficult to capture way, entwined. Because I want to do justice to their struggles and joys. Because, in my own way, and with all of my own projections and fantasies intact, I have fallen in love with them. To love the dead is for them to remain with you, introjected, present. Haunting and love are very close, indeed.

Abram Lewis, in his crucial work on the recurrence of "declension, addiction, paranoia, and delusion" (2014, 23) in trans archives, articulates a quandary produced by the recurrence of material that cannot be substantiated with historical proof or evidence in trans archives—for instance, transsexual philanthropist Reed Erickson's psychotropic meditations on the possibility of human-dolphin communication, or trans activist Angela Douglas's fascination with and speculation about extraterrestrial life, including "her discovery that a close friend was a nonhuman being, seemingly alien but possibly Satan, with 'grey reptilian, leathery skin, hairless, with coal black eyes,' that had come to earth to help transsexuals" (Lewis 2014, 23). The frequency with which such evidence of cognitive divergence, mental illness, substance abuse, and addiction appears is an archival testament to the institutional and interpersonal violence within which trans subjects were and are forced to build lifeworlds. This material, as Lewis writes, is "by no means easily disentangled from accounts of living in a violently transphobic capitalist order" (24). However, the dominant genres of historical narration would have us consign all of this material to the level of the anecdotal—unprovable, irrational, and thus subsidiary to the historical record. Perhaps it might be utilized as proof of mental illness. In its most pernicious form, this would serve to discredit the testimony and traces left by the subject in question; at best, it would be considered epiphenomenal to the historically substantive material in the archive. Historically speaking, trans subjects are already often considered infelicitous, mentally ill, disordered, or "crazy" by virtue of our transness alone; within a transphobic imaginary, these traces only further entrench that perception, rendering the archives we do have marginal, unreliable, and thus easily dismissed. It also presents difficulties for those of us who bear a debt to these lives, who are in a kind of transtemporal solidarity, who feel a deep responsibility to this material. This responsibility entails an ethical obligation to narrate justly, which is indeed challenging, given the aleatory, multigenre inventive speculation so manifest in trans archives. To care for these archives, to care for these lives, means, minimally, "cultivating openness to irreducible alterity" (Lewis 2014, 29), admitting that there are unknowable dimensions to our entanglements. This necessitates a historical witnessing in excess of a logic of succession, clear precedent and antecedent. We are related to these subjects in some way, yes, but it is not an inheritance, not a lineage. These people are not our "transcestors"—that word we sometimes use to position ourselves in relation to the pantheon of repeatedly memorialized trans subjects—but they are nevertheless deeply implicated in our current conditions of possibility.

The spectrum is built of specters that undo and exceed it.

So are we.

# Trans Care within and against the Medical-Industrial Complex

### Denials of Care

The nexus of care most commonly associated with transness—that provided by the medical-industrial complex—has often offered not much more than cold comfort to those trans subjects seeking it. Economically inaccessible, geographically dispersed, and rigorously gatekept, access to those gender-confirming surgical procedures offered by physicians have been, for quite a long time, an indicator of relative privilege, most commonly open to White, well-educated subjects of considerable economic means. While the hard-fought and ongoing battles that have resulted in recent expansions in transition-related insurance coverage and (imperfectly) democratized access to hormones have shifted this terrain considerably, the legacy of gatekeeping persists into the present, as does the high out-of-pocket cost of surgery for those subjects not enrolled in an inclusive insurance program, who don't have insurance, or who utilize Medicaid and live in a state whose Medicaid policies contain specific trans exclusions.

The fact that the subjects that populate trans archives are implicated in our ongoing survival is made abundantly clear by the traces of medical contestation they've left. The battle to end medical gatekeeping began a long time ago, and the (still inadequate) representation that trans subjects have gained in the areas of trans healthcare and medical policy are both recent and hard won. The model of medical patriarchal benevolence that tracks from the era of Harry Benjamin forward has proven particularly recalcitrant—and trans folks have proven particularly ready to do battle with it.

In spring of 2018, I visited the Kinsey archives at Indiana University to look, specifically, at the materials associated with the Harry Benjamin International Gender Dysphoria Association (HBIGDA) and its later transformation into the World Professional Association for Transgender Health, the still-extant organization that has authored the official, widespread Standards of Care meant to guide medical providers in their providence of trans-related services. I wanted to understand, in greater depth, how it was that HBIGDA transformed into WPATH and became the transnational standard-setting organization that it is today.

It turns out that, in the 1990s, HBIGDA was struggling considerably to cohere and operate, in large part because certain well-known members of trans activist communities began to publish critiques of the extant Standards of Care, honing in specifically on the problems that attended the so-called real life experience (or "real life test") that mandated that trans subjects live in their "preferred gender role" for an extended period of time (ranging from three months to a year) before they are able to access hormone replacement therapy and gender-confirming surgery. A paradigmatic example of this argument comes from a contributor named "Cheryl B.," who wrote in to *TV/TS Tapestry* (which would later become *Transgender Tapestry*) in 1994 in order to point to the danger of the real life test for trans women in public, single-sex spaces, pragmatically pointing out:

During the real life test, a risk lies in the use of public restrooms. While some pre-ops may well as women, others may have some difficulty. The police may arrest the pre-op on the complaint of another patron. If the arrest occurs after 5pm on a Friday, she may be detained over the weekend in a men's jail. Like Dee Farmer, the offending TS may be exposed to unwanted rape and infection with HIV.

The danger only exists during the real life test dictated by the tyranny of HBIGDA. Although I have repeatedly argued this point with my therapist and with other experts, the dictate remains in force. (Cheryl B. 1994, 18)

This argument should be, at this point, deeply familiar, because a variation of it has had to be routinely remade in response to mechanisms of medical gatekeeping as well as the sustained effort to prevent trans people from accessing single-sex spaces, witnessed most recently in the spate of so-called bathroom bills that seek to mandate that the sex marked on one's birth certificate is the determinant for which single-sex spaces they may access. The logic of it runs as follows: institutionalized transphobia and medical gatekeeping entwine to produce a necropolitical cascade of effects that threaten the lives of trans people, and trans women of color most intensely. The rhetorical force of Cheryl B.'s argument derives not only from her own experience but from her reference to Dee Farmer, a Black trans woman who was repeatedly raped and contracted HIV while imprisoned at the federal penitentiary in Terre Haute, Indiana. Farmer's case against prison officials—*Farmer v. Brennan*—hinged on her assertion that prison officials knew that she would be especially vulnerable to sexual violence; it went to the Supreme Court, who ruled—in their historic first direct address of rape in prisons—that prison officials who fail to make provisions for prisoner safety in such instances can be held responsible for the ensuing violence. They argued that it constitutes a violation of the Eighth Amendment (the one that prohibits cruel and unusual punishment). This

ruling was not necessarily a victory for Farmer or for imprisoned trans people. There was no direct commentary on trans
experience—Farmer was repeatedly and consistently misgendered by the court, treated and referred to as male throughout,
and in much of the mainstream reporting on the case.

While the claim that this possibility for violence "only exists
during the real life test dictated by the tyranny of HBIGDA"
is overdetermined—certainly, trans women face violence both
before and after accessing transition-related medical services—
it does drive home the point that medical gatekeeping intensifies risk and compromises safety. This emergent critique of the
Standards of Care would ultimately convulse the organization,
resulting in the short-term in the composition of a trans-led
Advocacy and Liaison Committee that was consulted during
each subsequent revision to the Standards of Care and in the
long-term produced a standing ethics committee in WPATH
(led, as of 2020, by trans activist and author Jamison Green).
Importantly, the formation of these committees marks the first
time in the history of trans medicine where trans folks were
officially and actively consulted regarding the treatment they
received. It's a landmark moment for trans patient advocacy
and a crucial moment in the genesis of the push for depathol-
ogization.

Engaging in such struggle can come at a high cost. It's worth
mentioning that when I encountered this letter to the editor in
the archive, it was in the HBIGDA files because it had been pho-
tocopied and sent to Eli Coleman, the University of Minnesota–
based sexologist who was the founding editor of the *International
Journal of Transgenderism* and who, a few short years later in
1999, would become president of HBIGDA. The note scrawled
in the top left-hand corner of the Xerox reads, "Eli—is she one
of your pts [patients]" (HBIGDA, box 1, series 1, folder 1). The
location tag beneath her name is "MN"—Minnesota. I presume

that this Xerox was sent to Coleman by another medical specialist affiliated with HBIGDA, and it testifies to the smallness of trans worlds. It is a situation wherein medical professionals are actively reading the small handful of trans community publications and able to single out particular patients—those engaging in public critique and protest of medical gatekeeping—with ease. So much for anonymity and privacy. It also raises a red flag concerning the possibility of retaliation. What if a medical practitioner, displeased with such contestations, decided to actively withhold treatment? Discontinue their relationship with the patient? Given the paucity and geographic dispersal of providers, such a rejection might very well be tantamount to a full-on denial of transition.

This isn't far-fetched speculation. Such forms of retaliation indeed happen. Recurrently.

Denial can take many forms. One of the most heartbreaking and infuriating aspects of wading through trans medical archives has to do with the consistent appearance of letters from trans folks seeking treatment with limited funds, asking for long-distance diagnosis, or if sources of financial support for transition exist. One woman writes to Alice Webb, who ran a gender-affirming practice in Galveston, Texas, in the late 1980s, inquiring as to whether or not she can get "help at a low cost . . . via mail" (HBIGDA, box 2, series 4 B, folder 2) because she doesn't have money, time, or the ability to travel elsewhere for a consultation. This is but one example; such inquiries appear so often in Alice Webb's archives that she begins to use a form letter by way of response, one that states that no financial support exists and offers—if possible—information about local or regional trans support groups that the inquirer might attend. When a refusal of care is the best you can hope for, what do you do? Where do you turn?

Increasingly, we've turned to each other.

## Crowdsourcing Empathy, Building Solidarity

Each day, my social media feed is populated with crowdfunding requests for surgery. Often, it's for facial feminization surgery, which is nearly unilaterally denied coverage. Other times, it's a request for top surgery, from uninsured and underinsured trans masc folks.

Each day, my social media feed is populated with requests for rent money, for money to keep the power on, for funds to repair a car, or to fund some other necessary expense that ensures minimal forms of survival.

Sometimes, I can throw money at these requests. Sometimes, the most I can do is commiserate in frustrated empathy. Both of these responses are trans care praxis. We turn to social media for support that is simultaneously fiscal and affective, simultaneously practical (for advice about physicians, knowledge about underresearched side effects of exogenous hormones, about what clinics operate on an informed consent model, to seek legal advice) and ephemerally affirmative (to be told that we look hot, to bitch about quotidian transphobia). We hear so much about the purported echo chamber of social media, the way it has increasingly dissuaded political conversation across difference, the way it has contributed to intensified and polarized partisanship. This ostensible dilemma of the demos is structured by the assumption of a specifically dialectic ideal: that continual cultivation of political agonism leads to deliberation, compromise, and ultimately (at least provisional) consensus. Thus, the echo chamber effect makes nonpartisan consensus impossible, or, more hopefully, quite unlikely.

But what happens when your identity becomes a political wedge issue? From debates about "bathroom bills" to Republican outrage about trans-inclusive insurance coverage to continual fearmongering about the specter of trans women in sport, to continual conservative-led legal initiatives to reinterpret Titles VII and IX as trans-exclusionary, trans bodies and lives have been scapegoated again and again as a sign of the excess and irreality of the political Left. Then there are the debates about trans-exclusionary radical feminism currently convulsing the feminist Left and leading to forms of unlikely alliance between certain sectors of radical feminism and the religious right that we haven't seen since the height of the Sex Wars. In this cultural climate, the echo chamber afforded by social media might be better understood as a provisionary form of trans separatism that offers imperative reprieve. It's where we access forms of preservative love withheld in the popular domain, and too often scarce in our everyday interactions.

Sara Ruddick, in *Maternal Thinking* (1989)—a groundbreaking work in feminist care ethics—frames preservative love as one of the central acts of mothering, which is the relational position from which she derives an entire epistemology of care. It's important to note, as well, that Ruddick understands "mothering" to be a practice taken up by persons of any gender; rather, anyone who commits themselves "to responding to children's demands, and makes the work of response a considerable part of her or his life, is a mother" (xii). Preservative love is shorthand for all of those acts that keep a being alive and intact, and it is characterized by a specific response to the vulnerability of an other. It means "to see vulnerability and to respond to it with care rather than abuse, indifference, or flight" (19). It doesn't require a particular affective orientation—we don't have to be cheerful or enthusiastic about it, and we may indeed feel deeply ambivalent about such forms of care. Ruddick: "what we are pleased to call 'mother-love' is intermixed with hate, sorrow, impatience, resentment, and despair" (64).

Of course, only some trans folks are children, and not all trans people engage in mothering. But if you're a person of trans experience and involved in trans communities, you know that intensified forms of vulnerability and exposure to violence and debility continue to inform trans lives across age groups. In addition to this, transition also scrambles normative temporalities of development. We have "second puberties" well into adulthood; we have "big brothers" or "big sisters" mentor us through transition because, though they may be younger in years, they've initiated transition long before us. We sometimes come from childhood homes that did not adequately provide the forms of preservative love and nurturance that form the crux practices of mothering. Alternately, we may have these forms of motherhood reduced or withheld upon the revelation of our transness. This is all to say we remain in need of mothering (in the many-gendered, expansive sense of the word) well into adulthood.

Trans historian Morgan M Page has given us a golden rule as we navigate the spaces of social media, and it is deeply informed by the ethos of preservative love. The rule is simple.

"I do not shit-talk other trans people in public. If I truly have a problem that must be addressed, I speak to them directly" (Page 2020). She goes on to unpack what motivates the rule: the high incidence of mental health struggle in trans communities means that call-outs and online harassment sometimes translate to self-harm and suicide. In addition to this, the rising tide of antitrans organizing has made a practice of solidarity across difference increasingly crucial. We can ill afford to be locked in self-aggrandizing battle with one another. This is doubly so when we consider that the online spaces wherein we congregate—from the Yahoo groups and chatrooms of yore to the networks we inhabit on Twitter, Instagram, and all of the closed groups on Facebook that effectively operate as both support groups and skillshares—are the only trans-majority spaces to which many of us have access.

These spaces, despite their potential, often reify the forms of stratification and inequality that shape our experiences IRL.

Public health researchers Chris Barcelos and Stephanie Budge, in their recent work on inequities that manifest in the context of crowdfunding transition-related medical costs, point this out quite explicitly. While noting that crowdfunding medical care is a "response to health and social inequalities related to a dispro-portionate burden of ill health and lack of adequate insurance coverage for gender-affirming care" (2019, 84), and that very few trans crowdfunding projects meet—or come close to—their goal, it is nevertheless the case that "the majority of recipients were young, White, binary-identified transgender men" (84) and that relative success with crowdfunding is "related to having a large network of distant ties through which the fundraising page is shared" (86). The better networked you are, the more social media capital you have, the more successful your bid for funding will be. This means that crowdfunding favors folks with the time, the extroverted capacity for engagement, and an extant and well-received "brand." In other words, it makes health care access in the context of compounded inequalities tantamount to a popularity contest. As such, it is an intensifier of already-existing forms of biomedical stratification.

The work of Barcelos and Budge insinuates a broader point: that trans care can all too easily reproduce hierarchies of atten-tion, aid, and deservingness and that such hierarchies exacerbate and amplify inequities. Any care praxis worth enacting must be attentive to such tendencies to reproduce injustice. This ap-plies to forms of emotional support as much as it does to forms of financial support. Our energetic investments are subject to partage and apportioning, informed by economies of existen-tial valuation that we must struggle to be conscious of—and to undo. We are all subject to forms of structurally produced and enhanced ignorance and elision, and these forms of unknowing and inattention are exacerbated, as Safiya Umoja Noble points out, by the algorithms that inform how and what we encounter in digital spaces. As she writes, "racism and sexism are part of the architecture and language of technology," from Google searches to crowdfunding initiatives (2018, 9). This is why Barcelos, in another article on the inequities of trans medical crowdfunding, calls for a "revolutionary ethic" that would transform the way this practice operates (2019, 7). Building on the concept of "revolutionary etiquette" developed by activist and performance artist Annie Danger (Danger and Nipon 2014), he suggests that such an ethic would call attention to the necessity of crowdfunding as a flawed work-around for the unjust neoliberal distribution of health and wellness services. He writes that "employing this etiquette would mean foregrounding a discussion not only of the healthcare inequalities facing individual trans people, but also an action plan that centers redistribution of financial and social benefits. This etiquette would prioritize a decentering of individual, normative transition narratives in favor of a collective vision of transgender liberation" (Barcelos 2019, 7).

There must be a dual movement wherein we highlight the imperfection and complicity that characterizes contemporary forms of trans care praxis as we push for collective redistribution. We need to address what constrains care, what marks certain bodies and subjectivities as (un)deserving of it, and call attention to the epistemologies, systems, and technologies that contribute to such unjust apportioning, even as we must navigate them in order to get (some of) our needs met. Care praxis is always within and beyond; forever prefigurative.

## Coda

To end, a story: when I was a kid, in the abandoned space of my childhood (which is a story for another time), I met another kid, similarly abandoned, and we lashed ourselves together in order to weather the sometimes devastatingly bad storms of our youth. We were both becoming genders we were never supposed to be, and we found home together. We built these homes, first, in each other. We added rooms through our zine trades and our late-night instant messaging and our lousy bands and our parking lot hangs outside of dyke bars and punk clubs. We found a broader network of folks who were similarly trans and queer and broke and traumatized and disassociated and trying desperately to find one another. We encountered the concept of prefigurative politics—building the new world in the shell of the old—pretty organically, through the anarcho-queer imaginary that animated the margins of punk scenes during those years. We came to realize that we were doing prefigurative political work whenever we made space for each other within our psyches, within our homes, within those spaces that felt like way less than homes, and within all those institutions and collectives through which we circulated—some durable, some ephemeral. We both became "voluntary gender workers," in addition to all the other hats we learned to wear, doing trans, intersex, nonbinary, and gender nonconforming advocacy work wherever we happened to find ourselves. We raised each other in the vacuum of care left by the overlapping economies of abandonment (Povinelli 2011) that shaped our days. We kept each other alive. We mothered each other through it, even though we'd both wind up way more daddy than mother. Our webs have spun out from the juncture of that decades-long intimacy, which is not a center so much as one significant t4t nexus in a constellation of so many, some thicker and tougher than others. The pattern of care and witness that we provided for one another is indelible, and I'm beyond lucky to have cocultivated it at such a young age; it has made it that much easier to identify and reject connections that fail to be characterized by this kind of commitment to making space for one another's becoming. When I think of care, I think first of him, and this, and the way it raised the bar for every significant encounter and intimacy to come. This is about a certain kind of faithfulness and a certain kind of obligation: about what we owe each other. Minimally, it is this: a commitment to showing up for all of those folks engaged in the necessary and integral care work that supports trans lives, however proximal or distant, in the ways that we can. This, along with an acknowledgment that it is precisely the recurrent, habitual, and mundane practice of showing up that makes us less and less willing to inhabit a world where we don't show up, and where whole systems fail to show up for us.

# Acknowledgments

For the whole beautiful mess: the trans accomplices doing rad work within and beyond the academy, the vast interwoven trans and queer kith-kin in East Tennessee and South Florida and Indiana and Pennsylvania and all the other places I've been thrown, and especially those doing the hard work in the South, from the lowcountry to the ridges. For Aren, whose cothinking made it possible to work these ideas out, and for Greg, for giving us a capacious space to begin to do so. For everyone taking and giving care as best they can. For Jules and Zena, for reading this early, and so carefully. For Libby and Tobias, for everything.

We're impossible without each other.

# Bibliography

Aizura, Aren. 2017. "Communizing Care in *Left Hand of Darkness*." *Ada: A Journal of Gender, New Media, and Technology,* no. 12.

Aizura, Aren, and Hil Malatino. 2019. "We Care a Lot: Theorizing Queer and Trans Affective Labor." Syllabus for the 2019 Society for the Study of Affect Summer School.

Awkward-Rich, Cam. 2019. "Craft Capsule: Elegy." *Poets & Writers,* December 23, 2019. https://www.pw.org/content/craft_capsule _elegy.

Barad, Karen. 2015. "TransMaterialities: Trans*/Matter/Realities and Queer Political Imaginings." *GLQ* 21 (2–3): 387–422.

Barcelos, Chris A. 2019. "Go Fund Inequality: The Politics of Crowdfunding Transgender Medical Care." *Critical Public Health* (online first view): 1–10.

Barcelos, Chris A., and Stephanie L. Budge. 2019. "Inequalities in Crowdfunding for Transgender Health Care." *Transgender Health* 4 (1): 81–88.

Barry, Lynda. 2014. *Syllabus: Notes from an Accidental Professor.* Montreal: Drawn & Quarterly.

Barthes, Roland. 1981. *Camera Lucida*. New York: Hill and Wang.

Barthes, Roland. 2002. *The Neutral*. New York: Columbia University Press.

Berg, Heather. 2014. "An Honest Day's Wage for a Dishonest Day's Work: (Re)Productivism and Refusal." *Women's Studies Quarterly* 42 (1–2): 163–80.

Bettcher, Talia Mae. 2012. "Full-Frontal Morality: The Naked Truth about Gender." *Hypatia* 27 (2): 319–37.

Bond, Justin Vivian. 2011. *Tango: My Life Backwards and in High Heels.* New York: Feminist Press.

cárdenas, micha. 2015. "Shifting Futures: Digital Trans of Color Praxis." *Ada: A Journal of Gender, New Media, and Technology*, no. 6. https://doi.org/10.7264/N3WH2N8D.

Cheryl B. 1994. "Dispute over Real Life Test." *TV-TS Tapestry* 69: 18.

Cooper, Ashton, Loren Britton, Kerry Downey, John Edmonds, Mark Joshua Epstein, Avram Finkelstein, Chitra Ganesh, Glendalys Medina, and Sheila Pepe. 2017. "Queer Abstraction: A Roundtable." *ASAP/Journal* 2 (2): 285–306.

Dalla Costa, Mariarosa, and Selma James. 1975. *The Power of Women and the Subversion of the Community*. Falling Wall Press.

Danger, Annie, and Ezra Berkley Nipon. 2014. "Emily PostCapitalism and the Revolutionary Etiquette of Crowdfunding: A Conversation with Annie Danger." *Grassroots Funding Journal* (March–April): 11–14.

Diamond, Morty, ed. 2011. *Trans/Love: Radical Sex, Love, and Relationships beyond the Gender Binary*. San Francisco: Manic D Press.

Foucault, Michel. 1995. *Discipline and Punish*. New York: Vintage.

Gill-Peterson, Jules. 2019. "Feeling Like a Bad Trans Object." *Post45* (December 9). http://post45.research.yale.edu/2019/12/feeling-like -a-bad-trans-object/.

Girit, Selin. 2017. "Turkey: Zara Shoppers Find Labour Complaints inside Clothes." BBC News, November 15, 2017.

Gossett, Reina, Eric A. Stanley, and Johanna Burton. 2017. *Trap Door: Trans Cultural Production and the Politics of Visibility*. Cambridge, Mass.: MIT Press.

Grant, Jaime M., Lisa A. Mottet, Justin Tanis, Jack Harrison, Jody L. Herman, and Mara Keisling. 2011. *Injustice at Every Turn: A Report of the National Transgender Discrimination Survey*. Washington, D.C.: National Center for Transgender Equality and National Gay and Lesbian Task Force.

Haraway, Donna. 1978. "Animal Sociology and a Natural Economy of the Body Politic, Part I: A Political Physiology of Dominance." *Signs* 4 (1): 21–36.

Hayward, Eva S. 2017. "Don't Exist." *TSQ: Transgender Studies Quarterly* 4 (2): 191–94.

Hopper, Jessica. 2015. *The First Collection of Criticism by a Living Female Rock Critic*. Chicago: Featherproof Books.

James, S. E., J. L. Herman, S. Rankin, M. Keisling, L. Mottet, and M. Anafi. 2016. *The Report of the 2015 U.S. Transgender Survey*. Washington, D.C.: National Center for Transgender Equality.

Lamble, Sarah. 2008. "Retelling Racialized Violence, Remaking White Innocence: The Politics of Interlocking Oppressions in Transgender Day of Remembrance." *Sexuality Research & Social Policy* 5 (1): 24–42.

Lewis, Abram J. 2014. "'I Am 64 and Paul McCartney Doesn't Care." *Radical History Review* 120: 13–34.

Lorde, Audre. 1988. *A Burst of Light and Other Essays.* Ithaca, N.Y.: Firebrand Books.

Lugones, María. 2007. "Heterosexualism and the Colonial/Modern Gender System." *Hypatia: A Journal of Feminist Philosophy* 22 (1): 186–209.

Malatino, Hil. 2019. "Tough Breaks: Trans Rage and the Cultivation of Resilience." *Hypatia* 34 (1): 121–40.

Manalansan, Martin F., IV. 2008. "Queering the Chain of Care Paradigm." *The Scholar and Feminist Online 6,* no. 3. http://sfonline.barnard.edu/immigration/print_manalansan.htm.

Manalansan, Martin F., IV. 2018. "Messy Mismeasures: Exploring the Wilderness of Queer Migrant Lives." *South Atlantic Quarterly* 117 (3): 491–506.

Marvin, Amy. 2019. "Groundwork for Transfeminist Care Ethics: Sara Ruddick, Trans Children, and Solidarity in Dependency." *Hypatia* 34 (1): 101–20.

Maslach, Christina. 1982. *Burnout: The Cost of Caring.* Englewood Cliffs, N.J.: Prentice Hall.

McArthur, Park, and Constantina Zavitsanos. 2013. "Other Forms of Conviviality: The Best and Least of Which Is Our Daily Care and the Host of Which is Our Collaborative Work." *Women & Performance: A Journal of Feminist Theory* 23 (1): 126–32.

Money, John, Joan G. Hampson, and John L. Hampson. 1955. "An Examination of Some Basic Sexual Concepts: The Evidence of Human Hermaphroditism." *Bulletin of the Johns Hopkins Hospital* 97 (4): 301–19.

Moore, Stacy. 2018. "Billboard Carries Message of Love for Trans People." *Hi-Desert Star,* November 23, 2018. http://www.hidesertstar.com/news/article_ebf46daa-ef64-11e8-bb12-b7b5c2a507fb.html.

Noble, Safiya Umoja. 2018. *Algorithms of Oppression.* New York: New York University Press.

Page, Morgan M (@morganmpage). 2020. "This seems like a good time to remind people of the rule I gave myself a few years ago that has really helped me immensely: I do not shit-talk other trans people in public—if I truly have a problem that must be addressed, I speak to them directly." Twitter, January 2, 2020, 4:46 p.m. https://twitter .com/morganmpage/status/1212852732652077058.

Piepzna-Samarasinha, Leah Lakshmi. 2018. *Care Work: Dreaming Disability Justice*. Vancouver, B.C.: Arsenal Pulp Press.

Povinelli, Elizabeth A. 2008. "The Child in the Broom Closet: States of Killing and Letting Die." *South Atlantic Quarterly* 107 (3): 509–30.

Povinelli, Elizabeth A. 2011. *Economies of Abandonment: Social Belonging and Endurance in Late Liberalism*. Durham, N.C.: Duke University Press.

Puig de la Bellacasa, María. 2017. *Matters of Care: Speculative Ethics in More Than Human Worlds*. Minneapolis: University of Minnesota Press.

Raj, Rupert. 1987. *Metamorphosis Magazine* 6, no. 3 (May–June). Digital Transgender Archive. Accessed October 2, 2019. https://www .digitaltransgenderarchive.net/files/m326m182n.

Ruddick, Sara. 1989. *Maternal Thinking*. Boston: Beacon Press.

Sanneh, Kelefa. 2007. "Heartthrob Swooning and Concert T-Shirts." *New York Times*. June 7, 2007.

Snorton, C. Riley. 2017. *Black on Both Sides: A Racial History of Trans Identity*. Minneapolis: University of Minnesota Press.

Spade, Dean. 2019. "Mutual Aid Syllabus." *Big Door Brigade*. August 29, 2019. https://bigdoorbrigade.com/2019/08/29/first-draft-of-mutual -aid-syllabus/.

Stanley, Eric. 2011. "Near Life, Queer Death: Overkill and Ontological Capture." *Social Text* 129 (2): 1–19.

Strapagiel, Lauren. 2019. "A Beautiful New Billboard in Detroit Proclaims, 'Trans People Are Sacred.'" *BuzzFeed News*, July 19, 2019. https://www.buzzfeednews.com/article/laurenstrapagiel /detroit-trans-is-sacred-billboard.

Stryker, Susan. 1994. "My Words to Victor Frankenstein above the Village of Chamonix: Performing Transgender Rage." *GLQ* 1 (3): 237–54.

Sullivan, Lou. 2019. *We Both Laughed in Pleasure: The Selected Diaries of Lou Sullivan 1961–1991*. Edited by Ellis Martin and Zach Ozma. New York: Nightboat Books.

Tagg, John. 1993. *The Burden of Representation*. Minneapolis: University of Minnesota Press.

Wampole, Christy. 2013. "The Impudence of Claude Cahun." *L'Esprit Créateur* 53 (1): 101–13.

Wark, McKenzie. 2019. "The Sun Is the Size of a Human Foot: An Interview with Andrea Long Chu." *Public Seminar*. October 29, 2019. http://www.publicseminar.org/essays/the-sun-is-the-size-of -a-human-foot/.

*(Continued from page iii)*

## Forerunners: Ideas First

**Hil Malatino** is assistant professor of women's, gender, and sexuality studies and core faculty in the Rock Ethics Institute at Penn State University. They are the author of *Queer Embodiment: Monstrosity, Medical Violence, and Intersex Experience* (2019).